To Dance, to Live

To Dance, to Live

A Biography of

Thalia Mara

Carolyn J. Brown

in collaboration with Carla S. Wall

University Press of Mississippi / Jackson

Publication of this book is generously supported by the Bookfriends of the University Press of Mississippi.

Willie Morris Books in Memoir and Biography

Designed by Peter D. Halverson

The University Press of Mississippi is the scholarly publishing agency of the Mississippi Institutions of Higher Learning: Alcorn State University, Delta State University, Jackson State University, Mississippi State University, Mississippi University for Women, Mississippi Valley State University, University of Mississippi, and University of Southern Mississippi.

www.upress.state.ms.us

The University Press of Mississippi is a member of the Association of University Presses.

Jacket painting by Enrique Dorda (1938) and frontispiece photograph both portray Thalia Mara in *Romance*. Photograph of painting by Gil Ford. Courtesy of the estate of Thalia Mara.

Manufactured in the United States of America

First printing 2023
∞

Library of Congress Cataloging-in-Publication Data

Names: Brown, Carolyn J., author. | Wall, Carla S. author.
Title: To dance, to live : a biography of Thalia Mara / Carolyn J. Brown, Carla S. Wall.
Other titles: Willie Morris books in memoir and biography.
Description: Jackson : University Press of Mississippi, 2023. | Series: Willie Morris books in memoir and biography | Includes bibliographical references and index.
Identifiers: LCCN 2022059441 (print) | LCCN 2022059442 (ebook) | ISBN 9781496845306 (hardback) | ISBN 9781496845764 (epub) | ISBN 9781496845795 (epub) | ISBN 9781496845771 (pdf) | ISBN 9781496845788 (pdf)
Subjects: LCSH: Mara, Thalia. | Ballerinas—United States—Biography.
Classification: LCC GV1785.M258 B769 2023 (print) | LCC GV1785.M258 (ebook) | DDC 792.802/8092 [B]—dc23/eng/20230109
LC record available at https://lccn.loc.gov/2022059441
LC ebook record available at https://lccn.loc.gov/2022059442

British Library Cataloging-in-Publication Data available

To all my friends in Jackson: Thank you for a wonderful sixteen years.

With heartfelt gratitude to Leanne Mahoney and Carla Wall, whose belief in, support of, and contributions to this biography of a woman they both dearly loved cannot be acknowledged strongly enough. Thank you.

Contents

Author's Note

In June 2006, I moved to Jackson, Mississippi. During the very first week of living in my new city, my husband's company offered us tickets to the International Ballet Competition (IBC), an "Olympic-style" competition that occurs in Jackson every four years for dancers pursuing professional careers. Drowning in boxes and wanting to get my house in order, I was going to graciously decline, but a close friend, Brenda, from North Carolina, my previous home state, made me an offer I could not refuse: she would come to Jackson and stay for the week, helping me unpack if I would get her tickets to the IBC. She is a dancer and has been all her life. She had always wanted to attend the competition and knew it only came to Jackson every four years. I could not say no to that deal. Brenda arrived and we went to our first IBC.

Brenda attended every event that she could: rehearsals, classes, and nighttime competitions. I only made it to the finale, but what an impression it made on me. I wish everyone could move to Jackson during the IBC—there is no better first impression that Jackson can make on a newcomer. With the flags of over thirty countries flying from its columns, the fountain in front on full display, and attendees dressed as if they had just walked out of the pages of *Vanity Fair*, Thalia Mara Hall was simply stunning. I entered the auditorium and heard languages and accents from all over the world. I thought I was in New York City or Los Angeles. It was a global gala, everyone brought together by a love of dance, and I was absolutely overwhelmed by the beauty, the diversity, and the level of competition I bore witness to.

It is a memory I have cherished since moving to Jackson. I settled into my lovely new home in a neighborhood on the northeast side of town and into a house with a three-sided, glass-doored office that allows me to look outside while writing the books I didn't know I had inside me when I first moved here. Living in Jackson was like drinking an elixir. I enthusiastically consumed all the wonderful arts and literary events the city had to offer: I reread Eudora Welty and discovered Margaret Walker, and that reading led to writing, and I crafted biographies of both of these important Mississippi women writers.

My closest friend in Mississippi, Carla Wall, who also was at the IBC in 2006 (although we did not know each other then), gave me a gift after the publication of my second book, *Song of My Life: A Biography of Margaret Walker*: a photograph of three women from Jackson, two whom I have written about—Eudora Welty and Margaret Walker. The third was Thalia Mara. The three sat for a portrait and were photographed by Kay Holloway when they were all honored at a gala in Jackson in July 1998 for their artistic contributions to the city. Over the last few years, while looking at the photograph, which is framed and hanging in my office, I realized I had to finish what I started. I had to write a biography of this third important woman from Jackson, who has given so much to her adopted city. Thalia Mara brought the IBC here and so much more. She has left an indelible mark not only on Jackson but also, as I hope to show, on dance all over the world.

Carolyn J. Brown

Reflections on Thalia Mara

As someone who has always been an avid supporter of the arts and actively engaged in community and state organizations, I recognized a kindred spirit when I met Thalia Mara. It was also intriguing that, at age sixty-five (when most people are retired or thinking about it), she would move across the country to a place where she knew no one to start a new chapter in her life.

Over the next twenty-eight years as we worked together on arts and community projects in Jackson, Mississippi, I grew to respect and admire Thalia's intense focus and discipline and the impact she was making. A gifted dancer, teacher, and visionary, she was also a creative thinker who demanded excellence in all she did. She was passionate, sometimes fiery, and tireless in her work. She could outlast those far younger and wouldn't take no for an answer. When you worked with Thalia, you had to buckle up. Fortunately for all of us, she was also warm, funny, and compassionate; she was a good listener and a woman of faith. As a result, she had an extraordinary ability to get others to see her vision and join her in making it a reality. She believed the arts were for everyone and could strengthen and change a community. As this book reveals, she was right: her impact on the arts in Jackson and the entire state of Mississippi was unparalleled.

On reflection, I now see Thalia as a role model for living a full and productive life. She didn't dwell on the past but lived in the present with an eye to the future. And she remained connected to people and ideas up to the end of her life, giving generously of her time and talent. Her passion for life gave her a vibrancy that remains with us and continues to inspire us. I'm a better person for having known Thalia. I miss her.

Carla S. Wall

Thalia Mara and Arthur Mahoney performing "Jazz." Photograph taken by John Lindquist at Jacob's Pillow, Becket, Massachusetts. Lindquist was official photographer for Jacob's Pillow who was credited for photographing dancers outdoors. © Harvard Theatre Collection, Houghton Library, Harvard University. Courtesy of the estate of Thalia Mara.

Foreword

Thalia Mara has been recognized among her colleagues and peers in the dance world as a fundamental leading spirit of their art. Richard Philp, editor in chief emeritus of *Dance Magazine*, astutely described her as "a monumental pioneer in twentieth-century American dance. Teacher, writer, educator, performer, philosopher, historian, and advocate, Thalia's accomplishments in ballet were astonishing."

As her niece by marriage (Thalia married my father's brother, Arthur Mahoney), I was privileged to have benefited from her nurturing spirit when, at the age of seventeen, I came to New York City to attend the Pratt Institute of Art. Over the many years following, Thalia and Arthur came to regard me as their daughter, and I regarded Thalia as my mentor and mother. She remains my guiding light today.

Following her career as a performer, Thalia began to teach, direct, and write, and she came to recognize how fortunate she was to have gained all her training and professional experience from the very best of the Diaghilev era: starting with her teacher in Chicago, Adolph Bolm; followed by her teacher in Paris, Olga Preobrajenska; and then in association with Michel Fokine when she performed in the South American tour of the Russian company L'Opéra Privé de Paris and later in New York City as a performer in his ballet company.

Given this rich legacy coupled with her ongoing concern about the human condition and the quality of life and opportunities available wherever she resided, Thalia was doggedly dedicated to passing all of this experience on in its multifaceted forms, especially to the next generation of young people. According to Richard Philp, "[Thalia] felt that contemporary ballet had declined into sharp, cold movement, and she emphasized a return to lyricism, romanticism, and musicality . . . [in which] the expressiveness of the individual must be encouraged." When she opened the National Academy of Ballet and Theatre Arts in New York City in the early sixties, a lengthy article in the *Ladies' Home Journal* quoted Thalia as saying: "I want to develop a generation of American ballet dancers so advanced in every phase of their art that they will have something of value to contribute to the culture of the country," and "Thought is the most important part of any action; when thought deserts the body, the body is cold."

As these quotations attest, ballet was a pure expression of life to Thalia. She said, "Ballet is not nearly as physical as it is spiritual, more in the mind." She also stated that "to achieve the mastery of your body, you have to meet the most rigid discipline . . . and through that, your body becomes free. Dance is the only art form in which an artist himself becomes a work of art."

Thalia had a grand spirit from within that animated her; she radiated goodwill in all her ventures and to all who crossed her path. As one of her ballet students from the 1950s related to me, "Anyone who spends time around Thalia comes away a better person."

Leanne Mahoney

Thalia Mara . . . In Her Own Words

I discovered this two-page biography in a box with scrapbooks, old photos, letters, business correspondence, and other miscellaneous items that Carla Wall has been holding in good keeping since Thalia Mara died. It was written in August 1967, when Mara was teaching and constantly raising money for her school, the National Academy of Ballet and Theatre Arts. Even though it reads as if someone else is the writer (in third person), I believe she is the author based on its content, personal details, and tongue-in-cheek tone. This book is my attempt to expand on this brief biography, and, as much as I am able, allow Mara to provide a much fuller version of her life story through quotations found in interviews, personal documents, letters, and other sources.

from: National Academy of Ballet
200 East 56th Street

. . . about Thalia Mara
Founder and President
National Academy of Ballet

Thalia Mara, daughter of Russian-born parents, was born in Chicago, where at the age of 9 she was enrolled in the Adolph Bolm School of Ballet. Bolm, a graduate of the Maryinsky School in St. Petersburg, now Leningrad, formed a company in which Miss Mara later was a featured dancer.

In addition to her American training, Miss Mara also studied with Olga Preobrajenska and Nicholas Legat in Paris. She danced with several companies in Europe, and later in South America, the United States and Canada.

Her appearances included concert dance tours with her own program, solo parts in the Fokine Ballet Company and appearances in the Broadway shows, *The Great Waltz* and *Virginia*. She was a featured dancer at the Capitol Theatre and Radio City Music Hall.

At 18, while touring South America, she was stranded when the manager left the ballet company of which she was a member. She met an American, Arthur Mahoney, who returned with her to New York where they were married and danced together. They started a school to train dancers and appeared throughout the U.S.A. in concert programs.

After Miss Mara and Mahoney separated, she put most of her savings in the establishment of the National Academy of Ballet. She rented a large apartment on Central Park West, where she lives with the Academy's boarding students plus several cats and an aging and articulate parrot.

Miss Mara has been choreographer for performances at the Paper Mill Playhouse in Short Hills, N.J. and was director and principal choreographer of the Ballet Repertory Company, which between 1960 and 1963 gave a number of performances for the New York City Board of Education Higher Horizons Program and toured under the auspices of the New York State Council on the Arts.

From 1947 to 1963, she directed the School of Ballet Repertory in New York, which she organized for professional dancers.

She is the author of a number of books on ballet that are used extensively throughout the world as textbooks. With Vladimir Djury, director of music at the Academy, she arranged a recording of "Music for a Ballet Class."

Miss Mara is a petite brunette with sparkling eyes and a quick sense of humor. She finds that as the head of a school that attracts talented youngsters, she must be a psychologist as well as a teacher, taskmaster and headmistress.

"You learn to push some youngsters ahead, to catch up with themselves, and to hold others back to their own best pace," she says. "And you have to learn to concentrate on motivation, to bring the best out of each individual according to his own ability and temperament."

cc 8/67

To Dance, to Live

Elizabeth Simmons, age five or six, on toes, wearing butterfly wings.
Courtesy of the estate of Thalia Mara.

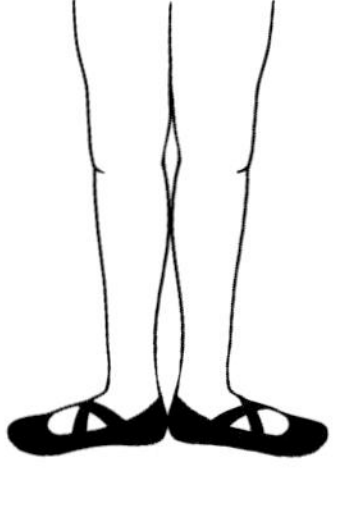

Chapter 1

Early Life (1911–1929)

This is hell, but I love it!

—Thalia Mara

Thalia Mara was nine years old when she saw the ballerina Anna Pavlova dance for the first time. "I was speechless for three days," she told interviewer Janet Baker-Carr over fifty years later. Pavlova was touring the United States during the early 1920s, and her effect on the public was similar to the impression she made on Mara: magical. Called "the most famous dancer the world has ever known," she left audiences absolutely mesmerized. Reporter Lillian Macdonald saw Pavlova dance in Houston the same time as Mara and wrote in

Above: "First Position (with accompanying illustration): heels touching. Legs opened outward at the hip so that the feet are turned out and make a straight line from the toes of the right foot to the toes of the left foot. Both knees straight." From *Steps in Ballet*, Thalia Mara.

Elizabeth Simmons's mother, Lydia Niminshinka, ca. 1920. Courtesy of the estate of Thalia Mara.

the *Houston Post* that "she is always something to remember . . . near perfection."

The year was 1920 when Elizabeth Simmons, later known as Thalia Mara, saw Pavlova dance.[1] Her story of being in that audience on that night for Pavlova's magnificent performance, however, begins much further back. She was born in Chicago to Russian-émigré parents named Semyonov on June 28, 1911. Her mother, Lydia Niminshinka,[2] born in 1892,[3] was from Saint Petersburg but left Russia during the early years of the twentieth century after becoming involved with a young Bolshevik group. Her relationship with this group posed a danger to the family and her father's publishing business; therefore, her father sent Lydia and her brother, who was two years younger, to London, where they had family.

Lydia did not remain in London very long. She and her brother immigrated to the United States and made Chicago their home. There she met and married Louis Semyonov, another Russian living in Chicago, but the couple was more commonly known as Simon or Simmons.[4] Their daughter, Elizabeth, was born when Lydia was only eighteen years old. Louis was in the haberdashery business, but when their daughter entered the first grade, Lydia went to work, too, as a seamstress. Because she was working full time, Lydia needed to find activities for her daughter after school. She signed her up for piano lessons as well as dance lessons with one of her friends from school. On the weekends Lydia and Elizabeth stayed busy taking in all the culture that Chicago had to offer: concerts, theaters, and museums. It was due to her mother that Elizabeth found herself in that auditorium that night watching the great Anna Pavlova.[5]

1. There is no consistency in the spelling of Thalia Mara's birth name: "Simmons" is the name in Mara's obituary and in the majority of articles about her. However, her birth certificate identifies her as "Elizabeth Simon"; her marriage license as "Elizabeth Symons"; her Social Security application as "Elizabeth Simons"; and her Ancestry.com page as "Elisabeth/Thalia Symons/Mara."

2. Lydia Niminshinka is the birth name of Thalia Mara's mother. On Mara's birth certificate, her mother is listed as "Lillie Newman"; on Mara's Social Security application as "Lillian Newman"; and on Mara's Ancestry.com page as "Lydia (Neminchinska) Newman." In Mara's obituary in the *Northside Sun*, a paper of Jackson, Mississippi, her mother is identified as "Mrs. Lydia Symons."

3. On another document, Lydia's birth year was listed as 1890.

4. Louis Simon was also listed as "Louis Symons" and "Louis Simons" on different documents related to Mara.

5. Lydia Niminshinka's backstory is provided by Leanne Mahoney, Thalia Mara's niece.

Elizabeth Simmons, age three or four, Chicago. Courtesy of the estate of Thalia Mara.

Elizabeth Simmons, age six. Courtesy of the estate of Thalia Mara.

Picture postcard of ballerina Anna Pavlova belonging to Thalia Mara. Courtesy of the estate of Thalia Mara.

Picture postcard of ballerina Anna Pavlova belonging to Thalia Mara. Courtesy of the estate of Thalia Mara.

Elizabeth Simmons could have either seen Pavlova and Ballets Russes perform at the Medinah Temple Auditorium in Chicago on Saturday, December 4, 1920; the Auditorium on Sunday, December 26; or at the Medinah Temple again on February 28, 1921. Whichever show or shows she saw, Simmons would have witnessed spectacular dancing: the programs for these three performances included Pavlova's signature work, "The Dying Swan," arranged by Michel Fokine; the pas de deux from Tchaikovsky's *The Nutcracker*; or Pavlova performing a variety of national dances from Hungary, Russia, and Poland. If she saw Pavlova dance "The Dying Swan" it would have been memorable indeed, as Pavlova had only debuted it in the US at the Metropolitan Opera House in New York City in March that same year. Dance critic Carl Van Vechten claimed the ballet was "the most exquisite specimen of Pavlova's art which she has yet given to the public." Pavlova would go on to perform it nearly four thousand times, and on her deathbed reportedly cried, "Prepare my Swan costume."

As a burgeoning young dancer, Elizabeth Simmons was enthralled by Pavlova. Simmons made her ballet debut on a Chicago vaudeville stage at the age of eleven as a performer in the troupe of her very first teacher, Miss Butler. According to Leanne Mahoney, Thalia Mara's niece, "Miss Butler had her troupe performing . . . ballet, so called, anywhere she could find an audience . . . on weekends; two or three shows a day." Thalia Mara recalled saying at the time, "This is hell, but I love it!" Her mother created most of the costumes Elizabeth wore in these performances and taught her daughter to be independent, showing her how to use public transit at a very young age in order to get to her dance lessons.

Elizabeth Simmons in fur collar and cuffs, seated (*middle*) on reindeer with friends at Christmas. Courtesy of the estate of Thalia Mara.

Elizabeth Simmons (*right*) on her ninth birthday with a friend, wearing hats. Courtesy of the estate of Thalia Mara.

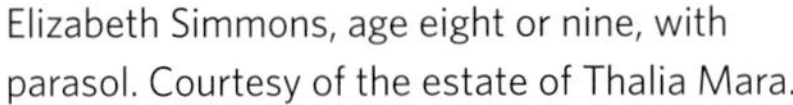

Elizabeth Simmons, age eight or nine, with parasol. Courtesy of the estate of Thalia Mara.

Medinah Temple program cover, Chicago.

Leanne Mahoney said it was a mother of one of the other students in Miss Butler's class who told Lydia that her daughter had "a great deal of natural talent" and that "she deserved a professional teacher." Lydia found legendary dancer Adolph Bolm, a graduate of the Maryinsky School in Saint Petersburg, to teach her blossoming ballerina, and she actually had Anna Pavlova to thank for it. Journalist Jeff Lyon provided a brief history of dance in Chicago that explained the connection:

> Through a twist of fate, the life of Anna Pavlova, by far the best-known dancer of her era, intersected with that of Chicago. The prima ballerina of St. Petersburg's Mariinsky[6] Theater left Russia for good in 1913, and her touring company found itself stranded in the U.S. in 1915 by the effects of World War I. . . . While Pavlova brought the beauty of her artistry to thousands of Chicagoans who otherwise might never have seen her, she also gifted the city with something else, namely [Andreas] Pavley and [Serge] Oukrainsky, two members of her stranded company who stayed on as co-matres de ballet and premiers danseurs at the Chicago Grand Opera Company. The pair were handsome and suave (Oukrainsky carried the hereditary title of Count Orlay) and they soon became society darlings. . . .

6. Both spellings, Mariinsky and Maryinsky, are acceptable.

Elizabeth Simmons (*top row, third from left*) in her first-grade class picture, Chicago. Courtesy of the estate of Thalia Mara.

Elizabeth Simmons (*second row, fourth from right*) in her eighth-grade graduation picture, Chicago. Courtesy of the estate of Thalia Mara.

Elizabeth Simmons, age eleven or twelve, when she studied with her first dance teacher, Miss Butler, Chicago. Courtesy of the estate of Thalia Mara.

> It was the Ballets Russes that gave Chicago Opera its successor to Pavley-Oukrainsky in 1922, when the renowned Adolph Bolm left Diaghilev for the shores of Lake Michigan.

It was under the tutelage of Bolm that Mara says in that same interview with Janet Baker-Carr that "[her] real education started."

Adolph Bolm was Thalia Mara's first introduction to the Russian ballet school. Bolm was a product of the Diaghilev era, having first joined Serge Diaghilev's Ballets Russes company in 1909. Here he was among a roster of other great Russian dancers: Anna Pavlova, Vaslav Nijinsky, and Mikhail Mordkin, as well as Michel Fokine as choreographer. Diaghilev was an arts impresario, and he envisioned a ballet company that combined elements of all the arts—music, painting, and drama—with dance. According to Edward Lockspeiser, "it became clear that conventional choreography

Elizabeth Simmons, age eleven or twelve, when she studied with her first dance teacher, Miss Butler, Chicago. Courtesy of the estate of Thalia Mara.

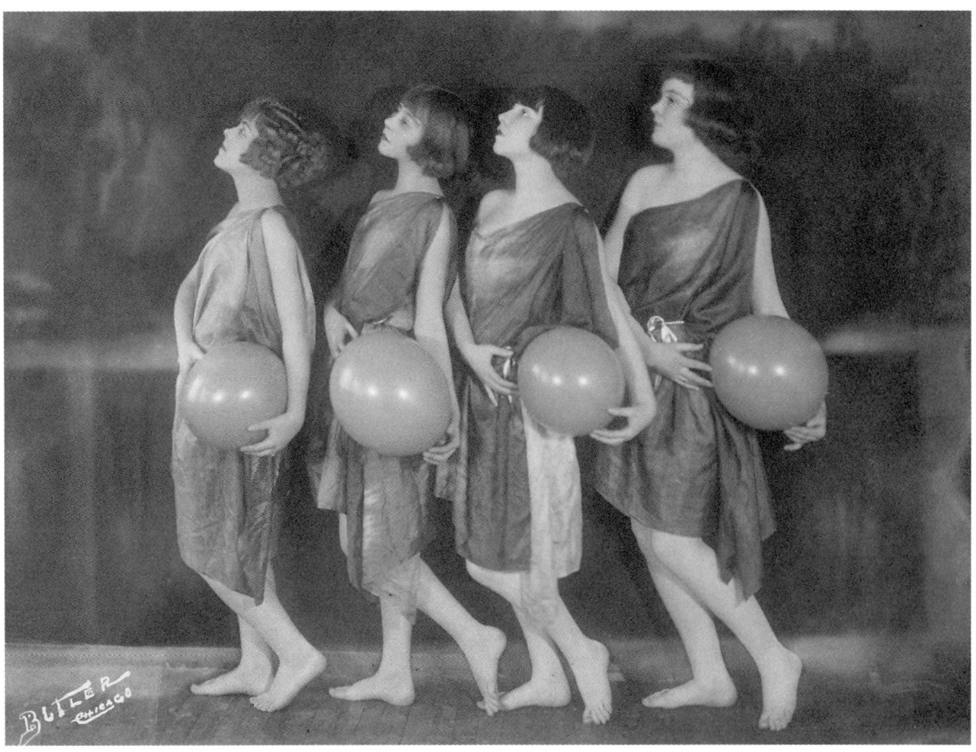

Elizabeth Simmons (*second from right*), age eleven or twelve, when she studied with her first dance teacher, Miss Butler, Chicago. Courtesy of the estate of Thalia Mara.

Elizabeth Simmons (*far left*), age eleven or twelve, in Miss Butler's troupe, Chicago. Courtesy of the estate of Thalia Mara.

Elizabeth Simmons (*far right*), age eleven or twelve, in Miss Butler's troupe, Chicago. Courtesy of the estate of Thalia Mara.

was to have no place in Diaghilev's novel spectacles . . . [and his] art reached its height in the three early ballets of young Russian composer [Igor] Stravinsky." With his ballet company, Diaghilev toured throughout the United States, Europe, and South America for twenty uninterrupted seasons (1909–1929). In 1916 Diaghilev asked Bolm to direct the first US tour. Bolm agreed, and the rest of the story is part of dance history: Bolm was injured during the 1917 tour and decided to stay in the US. He moved to Chicago in 1919 and opened his dance school at 624 South Michigan Avenue in 1923, continuing to work there until moving to California in 1929. Instructors at his school included such famous American dancers as Ruth Page and Anna Ludmilla (formerly Jean Marie Kaley).

It was into this world that Elizabeth Simmons entered in 1923 at the age of twelve. A fellow student, Josephine Schwarz, who also attended the Bolm School of Dance, donated her diaries and correspondence to Wright State University, and her ballet story is strikingly similar to Simmons's: seeing Anna Pavlova dance at Memorial Hall in Dayton, Ohio, inspired her to take lessons at a municipal school of dance. Her skill and desire quickly outgrew her local teacher, and, along with her sister Hermene, she began traveling to Cincinnati every Saturday to study. These weekly excursions quickly proved expensive; therefore, the sisters started giving dance lessons out of their home to earn money to eventually move to Chicago and study with Adolph Bolm.

The Schwarz sisters' letters to their family illustrate in vivid detail both the pressures and perks of learning from these formidable masters and provide a firsthand look into Bolm's studio. Josephine was seventeen years

Elizabeth Simmons (*second from left*) standing next to her first Russian teacher, Adolph Bolm, Chicago. Courtesy of the estate of Thalia Mara.

Sisters Josephine (*right*) and Hermene Schwarz. Courtesy of Special Collections & Archives, Wright State University.

Sisters Josephine (*left*) and Hermene Schwarz. Courtesy of Special Collections & Archives, Wright State University.

old at the time of this first letter.[7] She described ballerina/instructor Ruth Page[8] with awe: "Ruth Page works in class every day with us & talks about strength. I've never seen any one do a day like she does. Of course that is her long suit so naturally its good. She has signed a contract with the Metropolitan Opera & will start her engagement next January. Oh yes, she is naturally the Premiere Danseuse." Another instructor she simply called "Madame" and wrote:

> Dear old madame is trying to make someone do something right & I guess they can't. She certainly is feeling pretty strongly about it. She works so hard & the girls just can't do it likes she wants them. She's a marvelous teacher but her English is so very scanty that one has to guess a great deal just what she means & if your not used to it it's quite difficult to get along in class unless you stay way in the back & make a pretence of doing marvelous feats like slipping off of your feet or doing the Charleston with your ribs or trying to fly like an elephant & still look gracefull. Must close as no more room on paper.
>
> Heaps of Love dears
> As ever Jo

---

7. Please note that the original text of the letters is preserved, which may include errors and variant spellings.

8. Ruth Page "was one of the first Americans to dance with Anna Pavlova, and in 1925 was the first American to join Diaghilev's Ballets Russes."

1925 program for Ravinia.

Josephine Schwarz's letters also related what all the dancers hoped to achieve coming out of Bolm's studio: a place at Ravinia, which was located in Highland Park (right outside Chicago) and was known as the "summer opera capital of the world" from 1919 through 1931.[9] Every summer, dancers in Bolm's studio were chosen to dance in these operatic performances. In 1925, when Josephine was seventeen and writing to her mother about her hopes of earning a place among the cast at Ravinia, Elizabeth Simmons, age fourteen, was already there, dancing under the supervision and as a member of the dance company of the legendary Ruth Page. Josephine's older sister, Hermene, also desired a place at Ravinia, and she earned one alongside Simmons during the summer of 1925. In a letter to her family, she described the positives and negatives of being on stage at Ravinia:

> Dearest family——
>
> Last night I "suped" in *Lohengrin* and had the first real thrill of my whole life as far as beautiful people and marvelous voices are concerned—Alice Gentle was the queen and Rethberg was the Princess Elsie—Johnson was Lohengrin and D'Angelo—DeFrere and someone who's name I cannot recall carried the minor roles of the two Kings.[10]—Yours truly was a page in back of the King and held his sword and stood untill my two feet went to sleep and a lovely mosquito feasted off of my right leg and feasted so long and so hard that there are five bites in a row and they are swollen and turning black and blue from my scratching them. . . .

9. According to the article "The History of Ravinia," Ravinia "welcom[ed] to its stage the most-celebrated singers from Europe who sailed to America to perform at the Met and were in no hurry to make the arduous return voyage."

10. Alice Gentle (1885–1958) was an American operatic soprano. Elisabeth Rethberg (1894–1976) was a German American soprano. Edward Johnson was a Canadian operatic tenor (1878–1959) who often performed the title role.

> The opera was perfectly glorious; I have never seen anyone so very beautiful as Rethberg and Johnson is the kindest thing and the most ardent lover that I have ever seen in close action. I carried his crwon off the stage I want you to know. . . . Johnson sang and spoke so clearly (altho he spit all over Rethberg every once in a while in a close up but we decided it was because of his rolled rrrr's and tttt's.) . . .
>
> Loads of love as ever
> Hermene

Dancing outside and close to the leads, as Hermene recounted, was not always what it appeared to the audience. The heat and humidity were often intense. Josephine also finally earned a spot in the cast of dancers, and her enthusiasm for the role was quickly dampened (literally!) as she expressed in a letter to her brother:

> Dearest Brother—
>
> One time it was 100 in the shade & I & Herm had to dance; it was atrocious. All the girls were wilted & anything you put in your stomach made you feel goofy so I hardly ate that day & the next. But the days that are the worst are the sultry, hot, sticky, days when the air has so much moisture it cannot hold any more & your perspiration doesn't dry off at all.

Ballerina and dance teacher Ruth Page, signed photograph to Elizabeth Simmons: "To Elizabeth with lots of love and pleasant memories from Ruth Page." Courtesy of the estate of Thalia Mara.

Ballerina and dance teacher Ruth Page, signed photograph to Elizabeth Simmons: "To my dear Lizzy, a most talented dancer, affectionately Ruth Page." Photograph by G. Maillard Kesslère, B.P. Courtesy of the estate of Thalia Mara.

But despite the heat, the girls were giddy over their Ravinia experience and their lessons at the Bolm studio. They met the legendary Adolph Bolm, who often traveled due to dance engagements. Josephine reported to her brother in this same letter that "he looks just like his pictures. He was perfectly lovely & was so jolly & nice & talked to us a while after our lesson." He didn't teach the girls often himself, and Josephine wrote that she longed "for the day when he will first take a class."

Elizabeth Simmons studied for three years at the Bolm studio and danced as a full member of Adolph Bolm's company, Ballet Intime, as well as performed at the Chicago Opera Ballet at Ravinia Park under director Ruth Page. One of the highlights of her summer performances at Ravinia was, at age fifteen, being among the corps of dancers in the major flamenco number included in Manuel de Falla's opera *La vida breve*.[11] Soon after this performance, Bolm convinced Lydia that Elizabeth's next stop in her dance education needed to be Europe. She was only sixteen years old. Mara remembered her mother did not object but sent her alone by train from Chicago to New York and then by ship from New York to the port of Le Havre. According to niece Leanne Mahoney, the journey from Chicago to France was the first of many exciting travel stories for Mara:

> Thalia told me that when she got off the train in NYC, she had to find a hotel room for the night, as the ship to Le Havre departed the following day. An older man on the train offered to help her find that hotel room; however, she politely declined the offer! Once on the ship, however, she met two young men, students at Princeton, who were off to Europe for the summer. She experienced a delightful social time with them and they literally "danced their way across the Atlantic!"
>
> In Paris she booked a small room in a hotel, a little garret on the top floor. Her first night there, desiring to practice her French, she wanted to have some tea so she ordered hot water to be delivered to her room. When the water was delivered, what [she received] was a full tub so she could bathe!

However, Elizabeth would not be alone in Paris long. Her mother would join her six months later, having left her father and sold the house.[12] Now in Paris with her daughter, Lydia found an apartment to rent for the two

11. Lucrezia Bori, Spanish operatic singer, was the mezzo-soprano for this performance.

12. Mahoney revealed that Lydia shared with her that "on [Lydia's] wedding night, she knew she had married the wrong man!" She never explained why, but she did say that he was "very gentle and loving to Elizabeth and Elizabeth was close to her father." In her mother's opinion, Elizabeth inherited the best of both her parents: her father's "loving manner" and her mother's "drive."

Elizabeth Simmons (*center*) on the rooftop of the Gaumont Palace, Paris, 1928. Courtesy of the estate of Thalia Mara.

of them. Mahoney stated that Lydia "found it difficult to negotiate being that she was a woman without a husband." But she persevered and found employment in haute couture. She remained in Paris with her daughter for the next two and a half years. In Paris Elizabeth trained on a higher level, with a discipline and tenacity she learned from her new instructors, and told interviewer Janet Baker-Carr many years later: "I came back a ballerina."

Upon arrival in Paris, Elizabeth Simmons's only admission paper to a dance studio was a note provided by Adolph Bolm to Russian teacher Olga Preobrajenska. Preobrajenska was a famous Russian ballerina from Saint Petersburg who joined the Maryinsky Theatre and was promoted to soloist in 1896 and later to prima ballerina four years later. She appeared in over seven hundred performances throughout her illustrious career. In 1921 she left Soviet Russia to teach in Milan, London, Buenos Aires, and Berlin before finally settling in Paris. For the next forty years Preobrajenska was one of the most famous teachers in Paris—her students included both Anna Pavlova and English ballerina Margot Fonteyn.

Olga Preobrajenska's studio in the Salle Wacker was where Elizabeth Simmons found herself in 1927. Under Preobrajenska's tutelage she learned character dance, a specific subdivision of classical dance, which is integral to much of the classical ballet repertoire. It is described as a "stylized representation of a traditional folk or national dance, mostly from European countries using movements and music which have been adapted for the theater." A good example of character dances within a ballet is the series of dances that take place at the beginning of Act III of *Swan Lake*, which depict the national dances of Hungary, Poland, and Spain. Czardas from Russia and Hungary, Polish mazurkas, Italian tarantellas, and flamenco dances from Spain are all examples of national dances that ballet choreographers adapt and stylize into theatrical versions for the stage to insert into the ballets as character dances.

At Preobrajenska's studio, Simmons discovered a remarkable teacher whose "great gift," Mara later described, "was her intelligence and ability to *analyze* [Mara's italics], not only the technique but also those refined details that developed artistry and the individual expressiveness of each of her students." Perhaps it was "Preo,"[13] as Mara fondly called her, whom she later modeled her own teaching style after; in class she described her as follows: "She was a rigid disciplinarian, maintained great authority, and commanded absolute attention. However, she also showed infinite compassion and kindness and lavished great attention on those students who were especially receptive."

Simmons was one of those "receptive" students and quickly rose to prominence; during the three years she studied with Preobrajenska, from 1927 to 1929, she was asked to join the Albertina Rasch Dancers;[14] L'Opéra Privé de Paris, where she danced under the direction of the great master Michel Fokine; and the Ballet Suédois de Carina Ari as a soloist. For the Ballet Suédois de Carina Ari, Simmons traveled to Montreux, Switzerland, in 1928, and she performed in the loveliest outdoor setting, flanked by dancers and flowers and framed by an ivy-covered arch. In 1929 she traveled to Buenos Aires and performed in the premiere of Fokine's *Prince Igor* with L'Opéra Privé de Paris. This performance of Borodin's opera was commissioned as a wedding present by the nephew of the composer Jules Massenet for his bride, Maria Koustnezoff Massenet, "the director and 'diva' of the opera company." In this production, according to Fokine's granddaughter, Isabelle Fokine, "Fokine incorporated the vigorous style and athletic steps of Russian folk dances. This particular piece revealed Fokine's talent for organizing large crowds of dancers on stage and transforming their previously ornamental function into a powerful

13. This term of endearment was noted by Thalia Mara's niece, Leanne Mahoney.

14. Albertina Rasch was an Austrian-born American dancer, choreographer, and teacher whose troupes became well known during the 1920s and thirties for their appearances in Broadway musicals and Hollywood films. Thalia Mara performed in two Rasch Broadway shows in the 1930s: *The Great Waltz* and *Rio Rita*.

Elizabeth Simmons (*far right*) with the Albertina Rasch Dancers, Paris, 1928. Courtesy of the estate of Thalia Mara.

Elizabeth Simmons (*third from left*) in outdoor performance of Ballet Suédois de Carina Ari, Montreux, Switzerland, 1928. Courtesy of the estate of Thalia Mara.

Arthur Mahoney and Elizabeth Simmons (*second and third from left*) sitting outside during European/South American tour, 1929. Courtesy of the estate of Thalia Mara.

dramatic force." Fokine, as ballet master of the troupe, would have personally selected Simmons and fellow American Arthur Mahoney, "knowing them as students of [Olga] Preobrajenska and [Bronislava] Nijinska," respectively.

Before their selection for the South American trip, Elizabeth Simmons and Arthur Mahoney had first met on Montparnasse in Paris at the Café du Dome, a gathering place for Americans, artists, and intellectuals in the 1920s. On a trip to Paris with her aunt in the early 1970s, Leanne Mahoney recalled spending an afternoon searching for this café, which Mara referred to as "The Dome":

> We conducted this search based purely on her memory going back to her student days in Paris. While we lingered there for several hours over coffee and a few "petite" bites, she told me that she, along with other American students, could linger there for hours, [and] also explained that back in those days, when it came to paying the bill, the waiter would just count up the number of little plates on their table and charge accordingly.

However, it was not in Paris but during this European/South American trip that Simmons became romantically involved with the man she would eventually marry: fellow dancer Arthur Mahoney. They would not wed

Elizabeth Simmons and Arthur Mahoney (*fifth and sixth from left*) in Argentine newspaper announcement of the arrival of L'Opera Privé de Paris (addressed as Opera Rusa) in Buenos Aires, 1929. The caption states that the company will perform Borodin's opera *Prince Igor*. Courtesy of the estate of Thalia Mara.

Photograph of Elizabeth Simmons for Arthur Mahoney inscribed "For Arthur, Remember—Elizabeth, Buenos Aires – 1929." Courtesy of the estate of Thalia Mara.

until eleven years later, but during 1929 a serious relationship developed between them, and Elizabeth bequeathed Arthur a stunning photograph of herself in costume inscribed "For Arthur, Remember Elizabeth, Buenos Aires, 1929." Mahoney recalled in an interview with John DeMers that it was on this South American tour that he and Simmons "were stranded in Buenos Aires when the company went broke. After a month they worked their way back to the United States." That's the short version of the story.

Leanne Mahoney reported that following a very successful performance of the production in Buenos Aires at Teatro Colón and "by the time the Opera company reached Rio de Janeiro," Jules Massenet's new bride "had found herself a new lover. Her dalliance became known to Massenet in Paris, [and] thus the funding for the tour was cut off." Simmons and Mahoney were stranded, and obtaining transportation home was quite an adventure.

They first went to the US consulate in Rio seeking assistance but were rebuffed by the American agent there, who said, "You kids come here, get yourselves in trouble and then expect us to get you out!" Leanne Mahoney continued the story:

> At the British Consulate they found a very kind and helpful agent who arranged the necessary passage on an American vessel; however, there was a bit of a maneuver involved with this arrangement. The booking was in "steerage" which was the very lowest class and was for the poorest of immigrants. As such, they were instructed, once the ship had departed from the docking, they should find the ship's purser, who would have been alerted about their circumstances. They followed the instructions, but the purser said he knew nothing of any arrangement!
>
> In steerage class, the men were always separated from the women and also were housed in the "bowels" of the ship. As such, these passengers were allowed out of their confining quarters periodically during the day so they

Elizabeth Simmons and Arthur Mahoney in front of sign at the Teatro Colón announcing the performances of Opera Rusa at the theater, Buenos Aires, 1929. Courtesy of the estate of Thalia Mara.

Elizabeth Simmons and Arthur Mahoney standing on balcony during South American tour. Courtesy of the estate of Thalia Mara.

Elizabeth Simmons and Arthur Mahoney (*third and fourth from left*) on gangplank of ship, 1929. Courtesy of the estate of Thalia Mara.

Arthur Mahoney and Elizabeth Simmons on ship, 1929. Courtesy of the estate of Thalia Mara.

> could get some fresh air out on an open deck. On one of these occasions, a couple days out of port, the First Mate of the ship was watching over these steerage passengers from an upper deck and took notice of one of the men, so sent an assistant down to find out what his name was.
>
> [It was] Arthur Mahoney.
>
> Turned out, Arthur's brother, William C. Mahoney (my father), had been a classmate of his while on a training ship for Seamanship! They looked very much alike! Following that discovery, the First Mate made a special arrangement which allowed Elizabeth to use an available cabin to shower and also arranged for both she and Arthur to be fed each day. However, this maneuver was always disguised, thus . . . a fellow seaman would be sent down to this lower deck, disguised as dumping the garbage overboard, [but] managed to actually deliver proper meals to them both!

Leanne Mahoney stated that she does not know how long their voyage took but added, "I do know that the ship did make stops at other ports along the way."[15] It was at one port, "north of Rio, Thalia acquired 'Pepo,' a spirited green parrot, who became part of the family for 50+ years."[16] Finally, safely back on land and in the United States, Elizabeth and Arthur would begin the next chapter of their lives and dance careers in New York City.

---

15. The ship was the *Southern Cross*; it departed Buenos Aires and arrived in New York on December 3, 1929.

16. The parrot's name is pronounced PEE-poh and was acquired in Bahia, Brazil. He spent his last years in Jackson, Mississippi, and, according to Leanne Mahoney, "developed quite a vocabulary over the years . . . [it] was like having another person in the home." See photos in the inserts.

Thalia Mara performing classical ballet. Photograph by Walter E. Owen.
Courtesy of the estate of Thalia Mara.

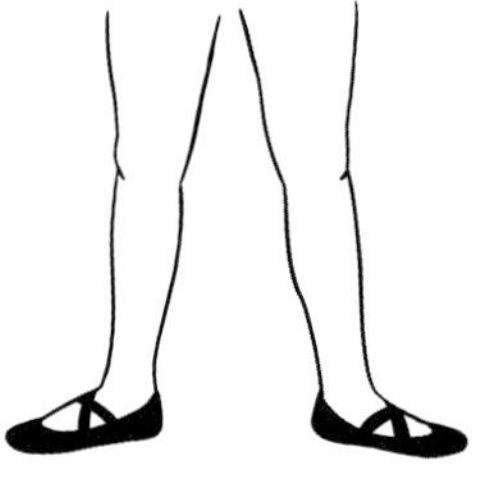

Chapter 2

New York (1929–1940)

I was grateful to have a job.

—Thalia Mara

Arthur Mahoney must have been a difficult man to resist. A former boxer, baseball player, and cowboy, he certainly had stories to tell. He revealed to writer John DeMers in a 1982 interview at the age of seventy-eight that "until he was 18, the idea of dancing as a profession never occurred to him." The moment was similar to Simmons watching Pavlova perform for the first time. He saw a picture of the great Vaslav Nijinsky in a magazine on a newsstand. "That finished me. . . . I didn't know who he

Above: "Second Position (with accompanying illustration): feet are about a foot apart, weight even over both feet. Legs and feet turned outward as in First Position. Both knees straight." From *Steps in Ballet*, Thalia Mara.

Arthur Mahoney, ca. 1929. Courtesy of the estate of Thalia Mara.

was or what, but I knew that the dance photograph was beautiful and that I wanted to be that kind of dancer," Mahoney stated in the interview with DeMers.[17] His father was strenuously against his son pursuing a career in dance—"You mean that fancy stuff on your tippy toes?"—and Mahoney ran away from his New England home.[18] He worked a year as a cowboy in Oklahoma, Texas, and Kansas, finally earning enough money to travel to New York City, where he studied ballet with Luigi Alberteri, ballet master at the Metropolitan Opera, "for six hours a day to make up for lost time." He then made his professional debut at the Metropolitan Opera at the age of nineteen and remained at the Met for three seasons before joining a vaudeville troupe that parodied ballets.[19] He confessed to DeMers that he felt like a traitor to his art, "but it paid [his] way to Paris." There he studied

17. The image was a cover photo of Nijinsky in the role of *Le Spectre de la rose*.

18. During his youth in Boston, Mahoney was a soprano soloist at Saint Paul's Cathedral and is remembered for having a beautiful voice. His obituary in the *Boston Globe* also mentioned he was a boxer.

19. He made his debut as a soloist at the Metropolitan Opera in 1926 in *La vestale* by Gaspare Spontini.

with his idol's sister, Bronislava Nijinska,[20] "and had the added thrill of dancing in the world premiere of Ravel's Boléro, with the composer himself conducting the Paris Opera orchestra."[21]

Photograph of Nijinsky in *Giselle* belonging to Thalia Mara. Courtesy of the estate of Thalia Mara.

Now back in the States, the couple found themselves living in New York at the start of the Great Depression. Elizabeth and Lydia shared a home. The first one was an upper-floor apartment in a small building in Greenwich Village. Leanne Mahoney remembered that "one night there was a big fire and Elizabeth, Lydia and Pepo were rescued by firemen who helped them down on ladders. . . . One actually carried Pepo down, with Pepo perched on his shoulder while Pepo made a loud, trilling, musical response of descending, all the way down the ladder." After this residence, they moved into a second home, an entire brownstone located on the Upper West Side of Manhattan, around 75th Street. Lydia rented the whole brownstone and then subleased rooms to various individuals, some of whom were performers. Often the tenants shared the evening meal together in the brownstone's dining room.

Arthur had an apartment in Greenwich Village, which he shared with two roommates. It was a three-story building located on 10th Street. Leanne Mahoney described her uncle's residence:

> The ground floor housed a thriving "speakeasy" known as Julius' cafe. I learned about this via stories my father told, when his ship was in port. He visited Arthur and spent a few nights there. In 1960, while an art student at Pratt Institute, I had my first big time New York date. Arthur took me to a performance of *The Fantasticks* in the Village, followed by a late night supper at a café known as "Dirty Julius," a very "in" spot at the time; its atmospheric décor included sawdust on the floor and cobwebs on the ceiling. As we lingered there, Julius' cafe came to mind, [and] it turned out [that] Julius' cafe had morphed into "Dirty Julius," the same old building with Arthur's old apartment above!

---

20. According to Leanne Mahoney, during Arthur's time at Nijinska's studio, he met British dancer Frederick Ashton, and both were caballeros in this production. Ashton would go on to be founding choreographer and later director of the Royal Ballet in London. Queen Elizabeth knighted Ashton in 1962.

21. Leanne Mahoney notes that many years later Mara would stage a more contemporary version of this *Boléro* for the Jackson Ballet Company. It was filmed by PBS and Mahoney designed the costumes.

Both dancers desperately needed to work, and, like the earlier vaudeville tour that Arthur Mahoney had said made him feel like "a traitor to his art," they found themselves, once again, forced to take less-than-ideal jobs in order to survive. Mahoney found employment as a soda jerk, while Simmons landed a job with the Capitol Theatre as one of the Chester Hale Girls because, she stated emphatically, "I had to eat." Chester Hale was primarily a choreographer of Broadway stage, screen, and ice shows. He formed and managed a Broadway chorus line known as the Chester Hale Girls. In an interview with writer Leslie Myers, Mara stated that "the 16 Chester Hale Girls danced from daybreak to 11:00 p.m. seven days a week for $60 per week. They danced four shows a day—except on holidays, when they danced five. They danced ballet, jazz, tap, character dancing, and even ballet on roller skates to pay the bills." Mara also recalled one memorable stunt that the girls performed:

> We had an aggressive promoter. . . . It occurred to her that if we could dance in front of the Chrysler Building spire, it would be a surefire newsreel item. . . . So a 16-by-16 platform was rigged up adjacent to the towering spire. The stage hung over the street—57 stories up. . . . It had

Elizabeth Simmons performing at Capitol Theatre in tutu on pointe, New York, 1930. Courtesy of the estate of Thalia Mara.

Elizabeth Simmons performing at Capitol Theatre, New York, 1930. Courtesy of the estate of Thalia Mara.

no rails—nothing. When [we] refused to dance on it, they decided half of us would go out. . . . Of course, it turned out to be my half of the line.

Thalia Mara, New York City, 1932. Courtesy of the estate of Thalia Mara.

And because she was the tiniest, Simmons was perched on the end. Mara later recollected, "When I think of it now, my knees get weak. We each took up a little more than a foot. We had little masks on—so we couldn't even see that well. And it was a windy day in March. So we went through our thing . . . with the newsreel cameras grinding away."

At least Simmons was dancing. Mara recalled in her interview with Janet Baker-Carr that it was a "very difficult time" and "[she] was grateful to have a job." She remembered having to do all kinds of things—"you had to be versatile!" She also felt that she needed a stronger stage name, and it was while in New York in her early twenties that she said good-bye to Elizabeth Simmons and became Thalia Mara. Leanne Mahoney said she made the name change because, "early on, during her search for employment as a dancer, she came to realize that she needed a more exotic name. It was also fairly customary at that time." Lydia was given the task of creating a stage name and chose "Thalia," after the Greek muse of comedy, and "Mara," which is derived from a name in Lydia's Russian family. Leanne Mahoney stated that "from then on Thalia Mara was not only her 'stage name'"; it was her "legal name."

In addition to working as a Chester Hale Girl, Mara danced at Radio City Music Hall as a member of the Radio City Music Hall corps de ballet and as a soloist. Radio City Music Hall officially opened on December 27, 1932, and Chester Hale was engaged as director of the opening show. At that time Mara took a job as soloist in the ballet at Radio City and performed in the grand-opening show. She stayed with Radio City for approximately two years. The corps worked four shows a day, 365 days a year, and Mara listed the famous American ballerinas Nora Kaye and Patricia Bowman as dancers among their ranks. Mahoney recounted her aunt describing dancing at Radio City Hall:

Thalia Mara and Arthur Mahoney in a Radio City Music Hall production, New York City, 1932. Courtesy of the estate of Thalia Mara.

Arthur Mahoney and Thalia Mara in Washington Square, New York City. Courtesy of the estate of Thalia Mara.

Thalia Mara and her mother, New York City. Courtesy of the estate of Thalia Mara.

> During Thalia's time the ballet dancers had to perform in every style imaginable—ballet, jazz, character dancing (folk), even ballet on roller skates! Sometimes in order to promote the movies, the "stars" would make a live appearance on the stage of the Music Hall. Thalia recalled meeting some of these "big stars," [and] among them were George Burns and Clark Gable. She said Clark Gable was really nice and liked hanging out in the girls' dressing room!

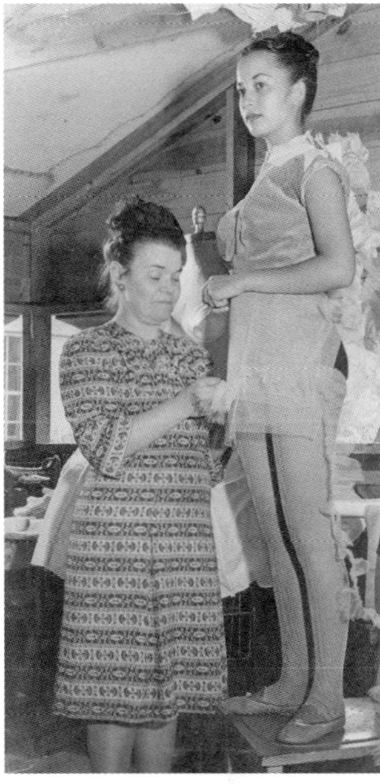

Thalia's mother, Lydia, fitting a mock-up of a costume on a dancer, Jacob's Pillow, 1947. Courtesy of the estate of Thalia Mara.

Arthur Mahoney performed in some of these shows at Radio City as well. Thalia's mother, Lydia, also worked there as a draper in the costume department, a job she gained because the artistic director and choreographer, Florence Rogge, admired the silk rehearsal tunics that she had made for her daughter.

Mara also danced at the Roxy Theatre and on Broadway in several shows. Both she and Mahoney persevered through this difficult period until they could return to dancing true classical ballet, and the opportunity presented itself for both of them soon after. In 1934 Mara reunited with Michel Fokine, becoming a soloist in his Fokine Ballet, and, in 1935, Mahoney joined the faculty of the Juilliard School as dance director and choreographer.

Fokine, of course, had collaborated with Serge Diaghilev. According to Isabelle Fokine, artistic director of the Fokine Estate-Archive and granddaughter of the legendary dancer, when the two first met in 1908 it was "a meeting that was to change both their lives and the course of ballet history." Diaghilev and Fokine were a powerful collaboration. Isabelle Fokine shared, "The impact of the first seasons of the Ballets Russes is hard to overstate. The influence it cast on the entire world of art, music, culture, fashion, literature, was unprecedented and is still a source of fascination to this day."

War and revolution would interrupt this successful collaboration and displace both men. Fokine came to New York City in 1919 when he received an invitation to work on a Broadway production of the show *Aphrodite*. It was only intended to be a short stay, but it turned out to be permanent, and Fokine remained in New York City for the rest of his life. Sadly, the two artistic geniuses would never reunite; Diaghilev asked

Michel Fokine. Used by kind permission of the Fokine Estate Archive.

Fokine to resume his work with the Ballets Russes, but Fokine declined, citing a debt that Diaghilev still owed him from their 1914–1915 tour. The two artistic partners never met again.

Fokine would achieve great things during his time in the States. Isabelle Fokine listed some of his accomplishments:

> In New York in 1921 he opened a ballet school that was to become a training ground for the first generation of American ballet dancers. By 1924 he organized his first company, the "American Ballet," which performed regularly at the Metropolitan Opera House, and toured the principal cities of the U.S. As well as staging his established repertoire, he also choreographed a number of new ballets over this period: *La Rêve de la Marquise*, *Igroushki* (*Russian Toys*), *Adventures of Harlequin*, *Medusa*, *Les Elfes*, and *Fra Mino*.

But Mara praised Fokine for much more. Fokine has been called the father of modern ballet, and Mara herself called him "the great genius of dance for the twentieth century." She had originally met him in Paris, and he was the ballet manager on that doomed tour in South America. She wrote that "all contemporary ballet exists based on the five rules for choreographers laid down by him." Entitled the "Five Principles of Ballet Reform," they are listed as follows:

1. To create in each case a new form of movement corresponding to the subject matter, period, and character of the music, instead of merely giving combination of ready-made and established steps.
2. Dancing and mimetic gesture have no meaning in ballet unless they serve as an expression of dramatic action.
3. To admit the use of conventional gesture only when it is required by the style of the ballet, and in all other cases to replace the gestures of the hands by movements of the whole body. Man can and should be expressive from head to foot.
4. The group is not only an ornament. The new ballet advances from the expressiveness of the face and hands to that of the whole body,

and from that of the individual body to groups of bodies and the expressiveness of the combined dancing of a crowd.

5. The new ballet, refusing to be the slave either of music or of scenic decoration, and recognizing the alliance of the arts only on condition of complete equality, allows perfect freedom both to the scenic artist and the musician.

She also credited Fokine with a host of other major changes in dance that were not as obvious. She told interviewer Janet Baker-Carr that up until Fokine, all ballet dancers wore "tutus and corset tops," but Fokine freed the body. Seeing dancer Isadora Duncan perform in Russia in 1905 inspired Fokine; Mara stated that "Isadora's insistence upon natural, ancient Greek tunic made a deep impression upon the young choreographer." Fokine brought natural movement to dance; he based it on breathing. He made ballet more musical and was the first to start using "good composers." He also was an excellent painter, and although he did not pursue this path as a career, he incorporated his passion for art into his choreography. All these elements—music, painting, and movement—were the basis of his "Five Principles of Ballet Reform" first presented to the directors of the Imperial Theatre in a 1904 letter, which also included the following statement:

> In place of the traditional dualism, the ballet must have a complete unity of expression, a unity which is made up of a harmonious blending of the three elements—music, painting, and the plastique art—dancing should be interpretive. It should not degenerate into mere gymnastics. . . . It should explain the spirit.

Sadly, according to Isabelle Fokine, the suggested reforms were met by the directors "with indifference." It was with Diaghilev that he was able to put his reforms into practice.

At the time Mara and Mahoney were in New York City, Fokine's ballets were attracting widespread attention. Even though some felt that Fokine's talents were being wasted in America—such as *New York Times* critic John Martin, who opined that "it is as if Beethoven were giving piano lessons instead of composing" —Fokine drew huge crowds to some of his performances. Isabelle Fokine reported that

> in the summer of 1934 a return engagement of the Fokine Ballet to Lewisohn Stadium caused a sensation. After 15,000 seats and 2,000 standees were admitted, there were still thousands trying to get in. The

Backstage at Lewisohn Stadium, New York, 1934. Thalia Mara in costume for *Schéhérazade* with Michel Fokine behind her. Courtesy of the estate of Thalia Mara.

police had to be called to control the crowds. On 8 August 1934 the *New York Times* had a headline on the front page that read "POLICE CALLED AS 10,000 TRY VAINLY TO SEE FOKINE BALLET AT STADIUM."

In this production of *Schéhérazade*, performed on the consecutive nights of August 6 and 7 at Lewisohn Stadium, Mara is featured as one of eight almees, or female concubines in a harem. Leo Boudreau described this striking production's inspiration:

> A leading feature in the appearance of Ballets Russes is the gorgeous color combinations of Leon Bakst, whose work was the sensation of art galleries and a dominant influence in the fashion world. He was the most distinguished artist in line and color that the theater had at the time. The beauty of Diaghilev's company springs from the costumes and scenery that Bakst designed for it. "Color should afford a joy for the eye," said Bakst.

In Fokine's 1934 showstopper production of *Schéhérazade*, the scenery and costumes, as much as the choreography, drew the crowds. And the program stated that these elements were "after Bakst."

In the late 1930s, Mara and Mahoney began touring together as concert artists across the United States and Canada, "performing ballet, flamenco, jazz and court dances of the seventeenth and eighteenth centuries." Leanne Mahoney described this period: "Arthur, who choreographed for them both, frequented the jazz clubs in Harlem, especially the Savoy, where Fats Waller played the piano. It was here that he learned the Lindy Hop. Thalia and Arthur brought it to the stage, incorporating it into their program finale. They called it the twentieth century minuet." Mahoney believed that it was at this time "Mara's dancing was at its finest." The couple graced the cover of the *American Dancer* magazine, a forerunner of the later *Dance Magazine*, as flamenco dancers in 1938. Their dance partnership would become official when the two would marry in 1939.[22] Their first home

22. The marriage license identifies Thalia Mara as "Elizabeth Symons." The marriage license was obtained on May 15, 1939, in Manhattan, New York.

Thalia Mara and Arthur Mahoney performing "Blue Fantasy," based on the popular American "jitterbug." Courtesy of the estate of Thalia Mara.

Arthur Mahoney and Thalia Mara performing flamenco. Costume design by Marco Montedoro. Courtesy of the estate of Thalia Mara.

Thalia Mara and Arthur Mahoney performing "Jazz." John Lindquist Photograph. © Harvard Theatre Collection, Houghton Library, Harvard University. Courtesy of the estate of Thalia Mara.

Cover of *The American Dancer* magazine, April 1938. Thalia Mara and Arthur Mahoney performing flamenco. Costume design by Marco Montedoro. Courtesy of the estate of Thalia Mara.

Thalia Mara performing *Romance* by Michel Fokine, New York City. Courtesy of the estate of Thalia Mara.

Thalia Mara performing flamenco in *Alegrías* in a "bata de cola" costume. Courtesy of the estate of Thalia Mara.

Arthur Mahoney and Thalia Mara performing the "Jota," the national folk dance of Spain. Courtesy of the estate of Thalia Mara.

Thalia Mara and Arthur Mahoney performing the saraband, a classic court dance of the eighteenth century. Courtesy of the estate of Thalia Mara.

together was a large studio (one room, kitchen, and bathroom) located on Christopher Street in Greenwich Village. They lived there for ten years prior to moving to a more spacious apartment in Jackson Heights, Queens, and then later shared a home on Long Island.

Arthur Mahoney's nephew, Ed Mahoney, remembers visiting the couple in New York as a child with his sister. He shared his memories with Sue Lobrano, former director of the USA International Ballet Competition, in an email after hearing about Mara's death:

> Thalia Mara was my Aunt. . . . I do remember the love and kindness I felt whenever we came together. The attention that she showered on my sister and I when we were young has produced lasting memories. On one trip to NYC . . . Thalia had set up an Easter Egg coloring competition in her kitchen with everyone, including the cook and the maid, producing multicolored treasures. There were lots of laughs and lots of spills and, looking back, I think Thalia had the best time of all. There were many cats in the house, too many to count on ten fingers, and the kitchen was full of them.[23] The resident parrot sort of controlled the chaos that day by

23. The cats Ed Mahoney refers to include a big fluffy orange cat named Bing (for Bing Crosby) and two Siamese, Tchulla and Screamer. Tchulla lived to be twenty-one years old.

The resident parrot "Pepo." Courtesy of the estate of Thalia Mara.

Arthur Mahoney pretending to balance on cat. Courtesy of the estate of Thalia Mara.

Arthur Mahoney and Thalia Mara at home in their Jackson Heights apartment, New York City, with their cats, Screamer, Tchulla, and Bing. Courtesy of the estate of Thalia Mara.

> barking out orders and flapping his wings for attention. The Easter Egg hunt took place immediately after in the backyard. And as if that wasn't enough, Thalia had tickets to The Greatest Show on Earth, Barnum & Bailey Circus. . . . This may not sound like much, but to me it was one of the greatest adventures of my young life.

The couple, now married and settled in New York, would embark on the next phase of their dance journey: as teachers themselves and founders of their own school of dance.

Arthur Mahoney, Thalia Mara, and parrot on stairwell in their Jackson Heights apartment. Courtesy of the estate of Thalia Mara.

Arthur Mahoney and Thalia Mara in their Jackson Heights apartment in front of Christmas tree with cats and parrot. Courtesy of the estate of Thalia Mara.

Thalia Mara, age eleven, with tambourine, Chicago. Courtesy of the estate of Thalia Mara.

Thalia Mara on balcony during tour, Buenos Aires, 1929. Courtesy of the estate of Thalia Mara.

Thalia Mara in costume during South American tour, 1929. Courtesy of the estate of Thalia Mara.

Portrait of Thalia Mara. Courtesy of the estate of Thalia Mara.

Portrait of Thalia Mara. Courtesy of the estate of Thalia Mara.

Portrait of Thalia Mara. Photograph by Edgar D. Evia. Courtesy of the estate of Thalia Mara.

Thalia Mara in costume. Courtesy of the estate of Thalia Mara.

Portrait of Thalia Mara. Courtesy of the estate of Thalia Mara.

Portrait of Thalia Mara. Courtesy of the estate of Thalia Mara.

Three stunning images of Thalia Mara at Jacob's Pillow in Becket, Massachusetts, by photographer and friend of Mara and Arthur Mahoney, John Lindquist. In these photos, Lindquist exquisitely captures both Mara's beauty and strength. Note Mara's shadow evident in these images. John Lindquist Photograph. © Harvard Theatre Collection, Houghton Library, Harvard University.

Thalia Mara performing Spanish Jota at Jacob's Pillow in Becket, Massachusetts. John Lindquist Photograph. © Harvard Theatre Collection, Houghton Library, Harvard University. Courtesy of the estate of Thalia Mara.

Photographer John Lindquist captures Thalia Mara striking a dramatic pose in exotic costume and headpiece at Jacob's Pillow in Becket, Massachusetts. John Lindquist Photograph. © Harvard Theatre Collection, Houghton Library, Harvard University.

Thalia Mara on horse, Jacob's Pillow, 1947. Courtesy of the estate of Thalia Mara.

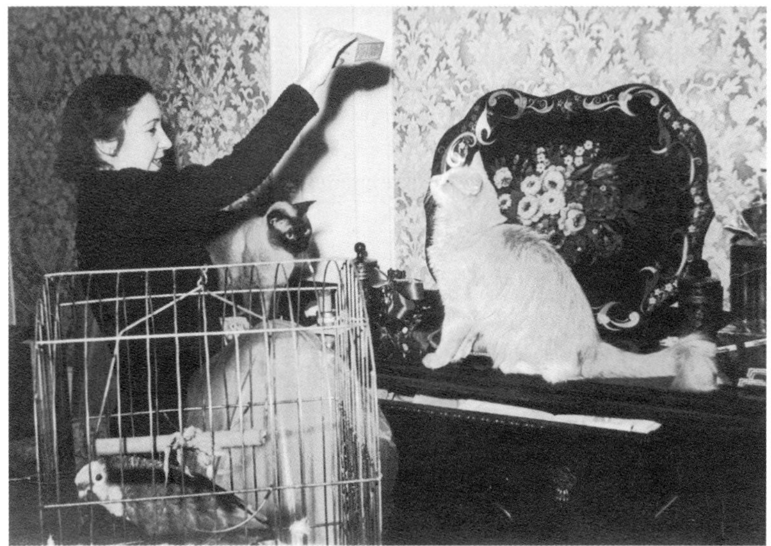

Thalia Mara with her cats and parrot, New York. Courtesy of the estate of Thalia Mara.

Thalia Mara feeding parrot, New York. Courtesy of the estate of Thalia Mara.

Thalia Mara, 1975. Courtesy of the estate of Thalia Mara.

Thalia Mara loved to entertain and is remembered for her wonderful parties and cooking. Courtesy of the estate of Thalia Mara.

Thalia Mara teaching single student at the barre at School of Ballet Repertory, New York City, 1954. Photograph by Lewis Goren. Courtesy of the estate of Thalia Mara.

Chapter 3

Teachers of Dance (1940–1973)

A good dancer is not simply somebody who can jump around; a true artist is a complete person.

—Thalia Mara

Thalia Mara credited her husband with the idea of starting a school of dance of their own. It was Arthur, Mara recalled, who thought if they were to have their own company, they should train the dancers themselves. "So he thought we ought to start teaching," Mara told interviewer Janet Baker-Carr. In this same interview, Mara shared her philosophy of teaching, one that she gained from her Russian teachers and time abroad:

Above: "Third Position (with accompanying illustration): both legs are opened outward from the hips, and the heel of the right foot is placed in front of the arch of the left foot. The feet touch. The weight is distributed evenly over both feet. Both knees straight." From *Steps in Ballet*, Thalia Mara.

> Well, of course, Europe is so different from America. Children grow up with the arts and every little town has an opera house or theater. In Germany and Russia and England, too. And they grow up with a knowledge of and love for the arts . . . [and] you can't be a dancer, you can't be a musician, without a lot of self-discipline. . . . To be able to express yourself artistically you have to have tremendous self-discipline to gain the technique because you're turning your body into a dance instrument. A musician can buy a piano or a violin, but a dancer has to make the instrument. And you can't do that without disciplining your mind and your will. Everything has to be under this very strict discipline.

It was this strict discipline and love of the arts that informed her philosophy of teaching and led Mara and Mahoney to open their first school of dance.

Mahoney, as mentioned previously, was an instructor first, having joined the faculty of the noted Juilliard School in 1935. In 1943, during his tenure at Juilliard, he was interviewed for the April issue of *Dance Magazine*.

Arthur Mahoney and Thalia Mara costumed for Spanish classical dance. Courtesy of the estate of Thalia Mara.

During the interview he espoused his philosophy of ballet and his recommendation on how to achieve style in dance. He said, "To acquire style, it is not enough to master the rules and imbibe the tradition, at the same time one must imaginatively relive the civilization that produced the style. The ability with which an artist can do this discloses the extent and depth of his artistic gifts." Both Mara and Mahoney effectively achieved this "style" in their performances, as they were widely praised by critics during this time. The *New York Times* wrote, "Though it is usually dangerous for anybody but a Spaniard to attempt Spanish dances, both Mr. Mahoney and Miss Mara emerged with flying colors." And the *New York World-Telegram* observed that "whether in solo or duets they showed consummate mastery of many national modes of dancing." Other papers called their performances "brilliant" and noted that "it is not often that dancers not Spanish born succeed so admirably in suffusing such typical dances with a genuinely Iberian atmosphere." There is no doubt, based on their mutual philosophies, performances, and technique, that the two were exceptional instructors of dance.

Arthur Mahoney and Thalia Mara leaflet, ca. 1940. Courtesy of the estate of Thalia Mara.

Mahoney followed his teaching stint at Juilliard with a position at Jacob's Pillow University of Dance, the famous summer school and dance festival associated with the University of Massachusetts in Becket, Massachusetts. The "Pillow," as it is fondly called, had an interesting history during the thirties and early 1940s. *New Yorker* writer Andrew Boynton explained:

> Jacob's Pillow was begun by the modern-dance pioneer Ted Shawn, who bought the land in 1931 and used it as a retreat for his company of male dancers; when they weren't rehearsing, they built many of the early structures on the site. (One of Shawn's intentions in forming his troupe was to change how people saw men who danced, and the works they created often incorporated robust, masculine movement, and occasionally resembled manual labor.) In 1933, they began giving "Tea Lecture Demonstrations" to the public, and continued doing so in the

Arthur Mahoney at Jacob's Pillow. John Lindquist Photograph. © Harvard Theatre Collection, Houghton Library, Harvard University. Courtesy of the estate of Thalia Mara.

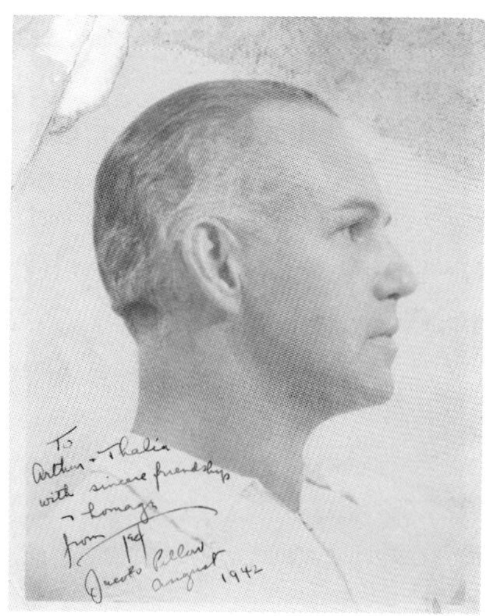

Photo of Ted Shawn inscribed as follows: "To Arthur & Thalia with sincere friendship & homage, from Ted, Jacob's Pillow, August 1942." Courtesy of the estate of Thalia Mara.

> summers up until 1940, when the company, Men Dancers, disbanded, and the members joined the armed forces. In 1942, a proper dance performance venue, the Ted Shawn Theatre, was built, and the Jacob's Pillow Dance Festival was born.

What Boynton omitted in this brief history were the years 1940–42, when founder Ted Shawn, deeply in debt, was forced to lease the property to others. In 1940 Shawn leased it to Mary Washington Ball, a dance teacher, who produced the Berkshire Hills Dance Festival on the grounds. The festival "was a financial disaster," but Shawn credited Ball with originating "the diverse programming that [had] become the Pillow's hallmark." Then, in 1941, Shawn leased it to British ballet stars Alicia Markova and Anton Dolin,[24] who, despite extremely difficult conditions, such as a lack of running water, put on the International Dance Festival there. It functioned as a school and summer residency for the participating

24. Sir Anton Dolin (1904–83) was a member of Diaghilev's Ballets Russes and founder, with Alicia Markova, his frequent partner, of the Markova-Dolin Ballet and later the London Festival Ballet, which today is known as the English National Ballet. In 1980 he was knighted by Queen Elizabeth II.

dancers, but conditions were bleak. The dancers were not paid; Caroline Hamilton reported that "many survived on $10 a week in unemployment benefits, contributing $1.00 a day towards food and lodging. . . . Dolin later described Jacob's Pillow as 'a summer of heart-aches, bills, work, lessons, rehearsals and headaches,' [but] despite wartime and gas rationing, people flocked to the festival for the weekend performances."

In fact, the International Dance Festival was so successful that enough money was raised by the board of directors to buy the property from Shawn, relieve him of his debt, and build a true theater for performances (named the Ted Shawn Theatre), "the first performance space in America designed specifically for dance." Shawn would remain director of Jacob's Pillow for the rest of his life, only taking a yearlong sabbatical in 1947 when he asked Mara and Mahoney to fill in. Thus, when Mara and Mahoney first performed at the festival during the summer of 1942, conditions had greatly improved; and a year later, when both joined the faculty, it was the beginning of a beautiful relationship—not only with the festival but with teaching dance.

In 1944, Mara and Mahoney were hired as artistic directors at the School of Dance Arts at Carnegie Hall. Their fame quickly grew during this period, and they were featured on the cover of *Dance Magazine* in January 1944 (see photo in color insert). Three years later their dream of directing and founding their own company came true: in 1947 Mara and Mahoney were appointed full-time artistic directors at Jacob's Pillow in Ted Shawn's absence. Their year as codirectors of the festival was especially noteworthy as *Life* magazine featured them in the August issue, and among the faculty that year was Joseph Pilates, who, according to writer Elizabeth McPherson,

> advocated a fitness method that balanced strength and flexibility with an emphasis on breathing and the body's "core," and often quoted the German poet/philosopher Friedrich von Schiller: "It is the mind itself which builds the body."
>
> While other exercise programs did exist at this time, Pilates's concept was a novel idea in the early twentieth century, and it particularly supported modern dance technique as it was developing in the United States. Notable dancers like Ted Shawn, Martha Graham, and Jacques d'Amboise sought Pilates not only for conditioning but also for healing. (Physical therapy as we know it did not emerge until the 1950s.) Those dancers who did not study with Pilates in New York may have encountered him at Jacob's Pillow from 1939 to 1951.

In an amusing remembrance from 2010, dancer Sharry Underwood recalled her first class with Pilates at Jacob's Pillow in 1942. She had run away from home to pursue her dream of becoming a dancer:

> At Jacob's Pillow University of the Dance, my first class was called Pilates. Pilates? Anxious, I went to the studio early and found a man standing on his head. "Gut morgen!" he called from the corner of the studio. He bounced down from his headstand and strolled over to me. Strength, solid strength, dwelled in this short, rugged but nimble man.
>
> "No no! You stay. Always start da day on da head. I am Joseph Pilates. You are new girl."
>
> He gripped my hand with a quick, numbing grasp. "Turn 'round! Turn 'round," he ordered, pushing on my shoulder. "Aha! Za back iss no gut!" Pilates gave a hearty laugh and with a couple of hard smacks to my upper arm, promised, "We fix! We fix!" . . .
>
> Pilates' class was compulsory for every student. We came willingly as we better understood how it strengthened us, gave us faith in our bodies. What I had called my "dancer's back" was a physical defect: lordosis. Under Pilates' care, I gave birth to three vertebrae I had never felt before, correcting my alignment. Joe was famous for correcting back problems, saying, "You are as strong as your weakest vertebra, like a ladder with a broken rung."
>
> Pilates' class was a fine warm-up for ballet, modern, Spanish—any dance class. Guest artists often joined our classes, as did our teachers, Thalia Mara, Arthur Mahoney, and Elizabeth Waters; sometimes Ted Shawn (founder of Jacob's Pillow) himself.

Joseph Pilates at Jacob's Pillow, from *Life* magazine, 1947. Courtesy of the estate of Thalia Mara.

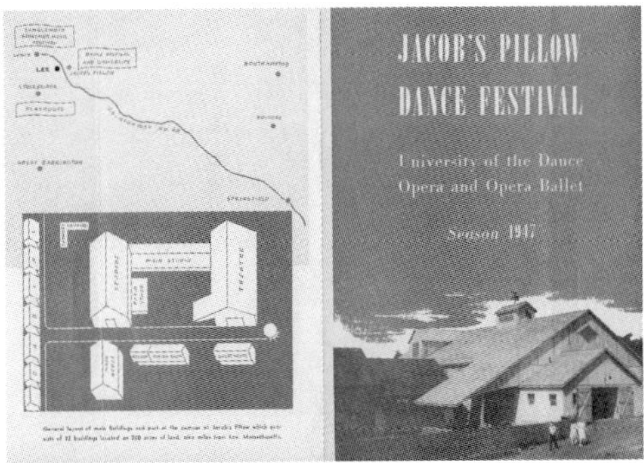

Jacob's Pillow brochure, 1947. Courtesy of the estate of Thalia Mara.

Postcard of Arthur Mahoney and Thalia Mara, managing directors, Jacob's Pillow Dance Festival, 1947.

From *LIFE Magazine*, 1947

DANCE

WHILE TEACHERS THALIA MARA AND ARTHUR MAHONEY UNCONCERNEDLY READ, FIVE OF THEIR STUDENTS STRIKE BALLET POSES ON THE VERANDA OF MAIN HOUSE

JACOB'S PILLOW

AN ABANDONED FARM ON A MASSACHUSETTS MOUNTAINSIDE IS THE SUMMER DANCE CAPITAL OF AMERICA

When Farmer Stephen Carter moved north from Connecticut to homestead just after the Revolutionary War, he settled in a beautiful spruce-scented tract in the Berkshire Hills near Stockbridge, Mass. Today Carter and his descendants have long since departed, but their farm buildings remain. These no longer echo to the stamp of horses but to the pattering of little bare feet as young ladies like the five shown above study dancing.

Carter's farm has become a dance colony, the summer dance capital of the nation. Its name is Jacob's Pillow, after a huge rock on the mountainside back of the farm. It is run by the husband-wife team of Arthur Mahoney and Thalia Mara, shown reading in the photograph above. This summer the Mahoneys, helped by a resident repertory company of 15 young professionals, have 44 students who are paying $500 each for an intensive eight-week course which covers everything from basic classical ballet figures to modern ballroom techniques. The students live in the barns or in log cabins, do all the housework and waiting on table, also help make their own costumes and scenery. They practice dancing incessantly, working under a series of celebrated dancers like Charles Weidman, Valerie Bettis, Iris Mabry, Iva Kitchell and Devi Dja, who visit the school in rotation and hold classes in their respective specialties. If the students show talent they are given parts in ballets which Director Mahoney puts on for public audiences once or twice a summer. Next winter the best of them will be dancing in Broadway shows.

CONTINUED ON NEXT PAGE 63

Life magazine, cover photo for the article that followed, August 11, 1947. There was a wonderful photo essay of Thalia Mara and Arthur Mahoney as directors of Jacob's Pillow in *Life* that summer. Courtesy of the estate of Thalia Mara.

Thalia Mara teaching ballet history at School of Ballet Repertory, New York City. Photograph by Jack Mitchell. Courtesy of the estate of Thalia Mara.

It was also in 1947 that, in addition to their work at the Pillow, Mara and Mahoney started the professional School of Ballet Repertory. For the next sixteen years this school thrived. Having lost their studio at Carnegie Hall, the two found a new location, which served as both a rehearsal space for their new performance company and as a center for training teachers. According to Leanne Mahoney, "Being that Thalia was a product of the Diaghilev-era Russian school, she was a fierce advocate for raising the standards of instruction. This training program took place during the summer in New York City. Teachers from all over the U.S. came to study and gain certification at the various levels." Mara's commitment to maintaining high standards continued with her founding of and election as president of the Ballet Repertory Guild, a teaching and certifying organization for ballet teachers that had the mission of setting standards for dance teaching in America, a position she held from 1951 to 1963.

Thalia Mara teaching Ballet Repertory Company class, New York City, March 1954. Photograph by Lewis Goren. Courtesy of the estate of Thalia Mara.

Arthur Mahoney teaching at School of Ballet Repertory, New York City. Photograph by Lewis Goren. Courtesy of the estate of Thalia Mara.

Thalia Mara teaching a class at School of Ballet Repertory, New York City, 1954. Courtesy of the estate of Thalia Mara.

Thalia Mara teaching Ballet Repertory Company class, New York City, March 1954. Photograph by Lewis Goren. Courtesy of the estate of Thalia Mara.

The decade of the 1950s continued to show Mara and Mahoney's commitment to teaching with the two dancers giving annual summer workshops to US dance teachers. Mara also taught at New York's High School of Performing Arts. Founded in 1936 by New York City mayor Fiorello H. LaGuardia, the High School of Performing Arts was created to provide a place where NYC's most gifted public-school students could pursue their talents in art or music while completing a full academic program. This teaching model greatly influenced Mara and would be the inspiration for the most important teaching she would do in her career: at the National Academy of Ballet and Theatre Arts. The establishment of this school would be the focus of Mara's life in New York from 1962 until forced to close in the early 1970s.[25]

This next project would incorporate the ideas of art and discipline that Mara had learned from her own dance masters and had seen firsthand at the High School of Performing Arts. In May 1960, in the "Teacher Says" column for *Dance Magazine*, Mara clearly articulated her philosophy of ballet and her displeasure with the lack of style of American ballet. She described the American style as a "mechanical approach" and called for a return to the old Russian masters:

> Forgotten are the great precepts of the art of ballet as laid down by such masters and reformers as Noverre, Blasis, and Fokine—those precepts which are the very essence of the art, and the very qualities which make ballet an art rather than a mere cult of physical movement.
>
> What has happened to the great standards set by Michel Fokine and the Diaghilev ballet fifty years ago? The ideal ballet dancer with brilliant legs and feet and fluid body and arms? The dancer whose body makes music, who is expressive, dynamic, lyric?

Mara blamed it on "the large classes, the lack of proper grading of classes, the disinterest on the part of teachers in individual problems, the lack of proper emphasis on *port de bras*, on *épaulment*, and on the use of the eyes and the head." For Mara, opening the National Academy of Ballet and Theatre Arts three years after this article was written felt like a calling, one that she deemed necessary to undertake.

When Mara recalled the opening of the school in 1963 in a later interview with Janet Baker-Carr, one can see that Mara's passion for these

25. Mara and Mahoney founded the National Academy of Ballet and Theatre Arts together. Mahoney did not stay long, however. Mara continued running the school on her own while Mahoney pursued other endeavors.

Thalia Mara and Arthur Mahoney evaluating students as guest teachers in summer session, Charlotte, North Carolina, November 24, 1957. Photograph by Ernie Shaw. Courtesy of the estate of Thalia Mara.

Thalia Mara and Arthur Mahoney evaluating students as guest teachers in summer session, Charlotte, North Carolina, November 24, 1957. Photograph by Ernie Shaw. Courtesy of the estate of Thalia Mara.

Entrance to National Academy of Ballet's second location at East 56th Street and 3rd Avenue, New York City. Courtesy of the estate of Thalia Mara.

ideals had not subsided. She declared in the most forthright terms, "As far as I am concerned, the arts are the basics of education, [which] is an old Greek idea. . . . The first thing educators do is take the arts out of education . . . and I think educators are totally missing the boat." She continued by describing the success she had at her school, the National Academy of Ballet and Theatre Arts, where art was put first:

> I had started a school like that in New York where the arts were totally integrated [in]to the academic curriculum. With history as the core, it was wonderful to see what happened with the children and how they developed and how they blossomed and how the kids who were not interested in reading learned how to read because they got involved and interested in what they were doing. And so I know what the arts can do in education for children.

The National Academy of Ballet and Theatre Arts was a school where students in fourth grade through high school could receive a complete education alongside extensive training in the performing arts. It also was one of only two such accredited schools in the United States, the other being in Washington, DC. The excitement regarding the academy's opening on October 1, 1963, was palpable; an announcement in the *New*

Thalia Mara teaching at National Academy of Ballet's first location on West 55th Street, New York City. Courtesy of the estate of Thalia Mara.

York Times stated: "An academic ballet school, the first of its kind in New York, will open under the direction of Thalia Mara. It is to be called the National Academy of Ballet." The article continued, describing the faculty and available scholarships:

> Incorporated under the education laws of New York and chartered by the New York State Board of Regents, the school will combine a college preparatory curriculum with a comprehensive course in classical ballet and dance-related subjects.
>
> The dance classes will be taught by Miss Mara, Arthur Mahoney, York Lazowski,[26] and Joy Macpherson at the School of Ballet Repertory, 117 West 54th St. The academic branch of the school, headed by Mrs. Frances Salzman, will be at 150 West 55th St. Tuition will be $1,200 a year. . . .
>
> Full scholarships for boys with or without previous dance training are being offered, and full or partial scholarships for girls with previous training may also be available.

26. York (or Yurek) Lazowski, formerly of Diaghilev's Ballets Russes, was notable for his many lead roles, including Petrouchka. He staged numerous productions for the Joffrey Ballet Company. Other impressive faculty members at the National Academy of Ballet included Vladimir Djury, former director of the Kiev Opera Comique; and Hilda Butsova, former member of Anna Pavlova's dance company.

In a proposal Mara wrote to establish a similar pilot school in Jackson, Mississippi, in the 1990s, she described in detail the philosophy and curriculum of the National Academy of Ballet and Theatre Arts:

> Working together with the teaching staff of the Academy, we developed a plan for a curriculum which would integrate the arts and the humanities into the traditional academic program. The humanities as we defined them for inclusion in this curriculum intended to create the "total artist," included intensive study of history as the record of life in various countries during notable historical epochs. It also included the history of music, fine arts, dance, theatre, and design, as well as art styles such as the baroque, classical, romantic, neoclassical, bauhaus, art deco etc.; the study of languages—principally French, as it is the language of ballet; literature as the basis, not only of our language, but as of great importance to other art forms in providing inspiration and ideas; the arts of painting, sculpting and drawing also of great inspiration to dancers.

Mara provided an example of this curriculum in practice: sixth graders focused on people of antiquity—such as Egyptians, Greeks, and Romans—learning about daily life, religious beliefs, clothing, food, culture, political beliefs, and even war. They combined this study with a visit to the nearby Metropolitan Museum of Art, which houses enormous collections of Greek, Roman, and Egyptian antiquities, and Barnard College, which puts on its own version of the Greek games.

Mara was completely invested in her new school, even opening her home to students who attended from afar and needed a place to live. Mara and Mahoney had been living in a lovely four-bedroom Dutch colonial house in Malba, a private community situated on the Long Island Sound, but also had an apartment in the city near their school.[27] Jolinda Menendez was one of those students who lived with Mara; originally from Trinidad, she auditioned and was accepted into the National Academy of Ballet and Theatre Arts. Menendez recalled, "Basically, I ended up being with Miss Mara from the age of nine until I graduated from high school. My mother took me to her and entrusted me to her full care. It was a big step. . . . Little did I know that Miss Mara would be more than a teacher. She saw me grow up and nurtured me as a little girl. I even lived in her home until the school had dormitories." Menendez credited Mara with her success; she went on

27. During Arthur and Thalia's time on Long Island, Thalia's mother, Lydia, lived with them, and niece Leanne Mahoney visited frequently on the weekends, as she was a student at the Pratt Institute. Mahoney stated that "this was when [she] first began working with Lydia making costumes."

Thalia Mara and Arthur Mahoney's home on Long Island Sound, New York. Courtesy of the estate of Thalia Mara.

to dance professionally with American Ballet Theatre and with companies in Europe. She stated, "Discipline, determination and commitment were only a few of the qualities that were the backbone of her school. Without the love and, above all, the spiritual guidance that she instilled in me, I would not have been prepared for life."[28]

Reporter Jack Metcalfe, who visited the school in 1968, shared his impressions about the students and curriculum for an article he wrote for the *Daily News*. He interviewed Thalia Mara, who told him that "a good dancer is not simply somebody who can jump around; a true artist is a complete person." Mara continued: "How a child behaves at the table, remembers to wash his ears, learns to follow a sensible diet, the way he enters a room to greet other persons—these are all parts of ballet." And Metcalfe wrote that he witnessed this philosophy in action: from the polite and courteous students who greeted him in the corridors, to the challenging classes in English, history, art, geography, mathematics, science, languages, drama, and speech, to the study of ballet for three hours every day, these students were immersed in a curriculum that rivaled the "great state-supported institutions of the London, Copenhagen, Moscow and Leningrad ballet companies." Girls were even required to take sewing

28. The Academy's enrollment included children of well-known performers of the time, such as singer Robert Goulet, flamenco dancer José Greco, and pianists Eugene List and Carroll Glenn.

Jolinda Menendez and Clark Tippet being coached by Anton Dolin in *Swan Lake* at National Academy of Ballet, New York City. Menendez was later principal ballerina with American Ballet Theatre and Munich Ballet; Tippet had a career as principal dancer and choreographer with American Ballet Theatre. Courtesy of the estate of Thalia Mara.

Jolinda Menendez, Clark Tippet, and Michael Wasmund rehearsing in Spanish classical style at National Academy of Ballet, New York City. Wasmund had a career with the Stuttgart and Houston Ballets. Courtesy of the estate of Thalia Mara.

Thalia Mara teaching at National Academy of Ballet, New York City. Courtesy of the estate of Thalia Mara.

Thalia Mara teaching at National Academy of Ballet's second location on East 56th Street, New York City. Courtesy of the estate of Thalia Mara.

classes ("a skill which is frequently valuable backstage") and boys fencing ("to build manly grace"). Graduates of the National Academy of Ballet and Theatre Arts either went to college and were fully prepared or became principal dancers in world-class companies, including the American Ballet Theatre, Joffrey Ballet, San Francisco Ballet, Stuttgart Ballet, Alvin Ailey Company, and the Bavarian State Opera Ballet in Munich.

Thalia Mara in her Central Park West apartment with National Academy of Ballet students. Courtesy of the estate of Thalia Mara.

April Berry, director of community engagement and education for the Kansas City Ballet, corroborated Metcalfe's account. A student at the National Academy of Ballet and Theatre Arts from 1967 to 1969, Berry attended for middle school, grades six through eight. She said in an interview with the author that "Miss Mara" was the "first professional teacher" she had and that she was completely in awe of her. Mara was extremely demanding and expected excellence from her students. It started with appearance. Berry recalled that even the younger dancers had to wear the same color leotards and ballet slippers, and hair had to be neat and tidy. She added, "We all had to wear our hair in two braids that we coiled into two ponytails that crisscrossed in the back. We also had to wear white ribbons. If we did not

Thalia Mara (*far left*) on stage with National Academy of Ballet students in San Juan, Puerto Rico, 1970. Seated at the table in front are the governor and his wife. Vladimir Djury, music director of the National Academy of Ballet, stands center right front. Photograph by Wagner International Photos Inc. Courtesy of the estate of Thalia Mara.

Easter performance in front lobby of Waldorf Astoria Hotel, New York City. *Left to right:* Michael Wasmund, Jolinda Menendez, and Clark Tippet, performing in classical Spanish style. They are all about fourteen years old. *Behind*, Irene Karolyi standing in costume. Thalia Mara always encouraged her students to perform out in public spaces.

have the ribbons, we did not dance and had to sit against the wall that day. Miss Mara was elegant and stylish and we were expected to be so, too." When asked if Miss Mara scared her as a young adolescent dancer, Berry said no: "I respected her, and everything I learned from her I still use to this day."

Berry also recalled frequent visits from reporters and potential donors to the school; "Miss Mara was constantly fundraising, and would invite potential donors to visit the Academy. We had to be on our best behavior at all times." The greatest gift that Miss Mara left her, Berry said, was a "beautiful and strong foundation" for dance and encouragement to pursue

Approximately fifty students in San Juan, Puerto Rico, to perform *The Nutcracker* with full symphony orchestra, December 1970. Courtesy of the estate of Thalia Mara.

her dreams. She continued, "When I had the opportunity to leave the National Academy at age fourteen and attend the Professional Children's School and dance with the Dance Theatre of Harlem, Mara did not stop me. She always said 'Seize your opportunity.' And she continued to follow my career, even sending me a note later, writing 'I am so proud of you,' when I joined the Alvin Ailey Company." Mara's mantra, "To live is to dance," still resonates with Berry today.

Despite much success—enrollment grew from twelve students in 1963 to one hundred in 1968—and Metcalfe's prediction that this was a "unique" institution that was "here to stay," the funding well ran dry and Mara was forced to shutter the school in 1973. She would not say good-bye to teaching, however. Now separated from Mahoney, who had moved to California in 1963 to pursue dance opportunities there, Mara would embrace the next chapter of her life with a move of her own.

Thalia Mara teaching student Beth Ware at Jackson Ballet.
Courtesy of the estate of Thalia Mara.

Chapter 4

Building Ballet in Mississippi (1973–1979)

People thought I was crazy.

—Thalia Mara

Two years after the National Academy of Ballet and Theatre Arts closed its doors, Thalia Mara received a most interesting invitation: to travel south, to Jackson, Mississippi, at the request of Cora Jeanne Miller, president of the Jackson Ballet Guild, and Ed Lydick, chairman of the board of the Jackson Ballet, to consider an opportunity to create a professional ballet company and school based on the foundation laid by Rex Cooper and his wife, Albia Kavan Cooper, former principal dancers with the American Ballet Theatre,

Above: "Fourth Position (with accompanying illustration): both legs are opened outward from the hips. The feet are about one foot apart with the right foot opposite the left foot and directly in front of it (heel of the right foot in front of the toes of the left foot). Both knees straight, the weight evenly distributed over both feet." From *Steps in Ballet*, Thalia Mara.

both of whom Mara knew. Rex Cooper was from Forest, Mississippi, and had returned to his home state to become artistic director of the Jackson Ballet. Sadly, he died in 1970 of cancer. The Jackson Ballet was in need of an artistic director and teacher for the young ballet company, and Mara was in need of a new home. A report, written by Miller in 2014 about the early days of the Jackson Ballet, told the story. According to Miller, Lydick was reading *Dance Magazine* in May 1975 and saw an ad that Mara had placed; she was seeking a new location "to manage a school of ballet and be the artistic director of a ballet company." Miller continued as follows:

> Ed Lydick called [me] . . . to come to his office and have a three-way conversation with Thalia Mara: and invite her to come to Jackson to meet with officers and board members of Jackson Ballet. They wanted to know if she would be interested in becoming the Artistic Director of our school and company and teach the advanced students.
>
> Thalia Mara came to Jackson in June 1975. The board of directors of Jackson Ballet hosted a dinner for her at the University Club, and [she] was offered and she accepted the job of artistic director for Jackson Ballet. The Ballet Guild hosted a luncheon for her at Colonial Country Club on June 12, 1975, and she was introduced to the ladies of the Guild. The first meeting of the Jackson Ballet board followed thereafter at the School of Ballet on Mitchell Ave. in Fondren. The board welcomed Thalia Mara as [the] new artistic director at the June meeting.

Mara recalled her impression of Jackson when she first visited in June 1975:

> When I was persuaded to come to speak at the annual luncheon of the Guild in May[29] of that year, I met many fine people, citizens of this city, civic-minded and all eager to provide a professional representation of an art they loved for the city they loved. I was much impressed by the beauty of Jackson and the sincerity of the people I met, the fact that the city supported a symphony orchestra, whose conductor served on the Ballet Guild Board, as well as an Opera Company and a Community Theatre group. When the chairman of the Guild Board said to me, "We want to go first class all the way; we want someone who will think big," my initial resistance melted and I went back to New York with the beginning of a vision.

Other factors weighed in on Mara's decision as well: she heard that a new art center was about to be built; the conductor of the Mississippi

29. According to Cora Jeanne Miller's report, the luncheon actually took place on June 12.

The Jackson Ballet Guild Inc.

Miss Thalia Mara

THE JACKSON BALLET GUILD, INC.
P. O. Box 4713
Jackson, Mississippi 39216

July 13, 1975

NEWSLETTER

Our exciting news today is that Miss Thalia Mara has consented to pull up her roots in New York City, and move herself, her life and her talents to Jackson, Mississippi.

Newsletter of Jackson Ballet Guild, dated July 13, 1975, announcing Thalia Mara as the new artistic director for the company. Courtesy of the estate of Thalia Mara.

Symphony expressed his desire and willingness to work with her; and the director of the Mississippi Arts Commission was eager and ready to assist. She also remembered being moved by the plight of the dance students:

> I thought it a great pity that talented youngsters had to leave Mississippi in order to receive the training and experience they needed if they wanted to make careers in dance, and that once they left they never came back, thus depriving the community of their talents. I reasoned that I could provide the training and experience here via the school, and that they would then grow into the professional company which would provide the career opportunities and livelihood they needed while contributing to the growth of the cultural life of the community. I also believed that by cooperating with the other arts groups we could, in time, turn Jackson into not just the "distribution center" for the deep South, but also its art center.

Shortly thereafter, Mara, age sixty-five, signed a five-year contract (she said, "I knew it was a minimum time in which to achieve anything") and was appointed artistic director of the Jackson Ballet. She could have directed a touring dance company of the Metropolitan Opera House but chose to come to Jackson instead. She told Donnie Snow in an interview, "I decided that I'd have more of an impact in Jackson. . . . So I moved here."

Thalia Mara teaching at Jackson Ballet. Dancer standing next to Mara is Beth Ware. Courtesy of the estate of Thalia Mara.

Thalia Mara teaching dance at Jackson Ballet. Courtesy of the estate of Thalia Mara.

It did not take Mara five years to create a professional dance company in Jackson. She recalled in a 2001 interview in the *Clarion-Ledger* with interviewer Sherry Lucas that "the first part of that first year was terrible." She remembered "stunned students who didn't understand her professional approach":

> I had to pin them down. . . . It was hard for them to take. They were used to flying around. . . . They weren't used to getting things from the bottom up. Afterward, they began to see.
>
> What a professional career teaches you is that everything counts. Every little thing matters. All the little things go to make up the one big thing.

She told Donnie Snow, "I was used to kids who wanted to be dancers; who ate, slept and lived dance. These kids wanted to be cheerleaders."[30] But by April 1976, just a year after Mara took the helm, the Jackson Ballet achieved Performing Member status in the Southeastern Regional Ballet Association. The original ballet troupe was comprised of twenty-four dancers (with only one male dancer, David Keary, among them), "with most being homegrown Mississippi dancers trained by Mara." Leanne Mahoney told the *Clarion-Ledger* that "as [the group] developed, [it] provided employment to many local dancers and musicians. The company was [later] engaged by Columbia Artists Management to perform outside

30. David Keary, a former student of Mara's, recalls a five o'clock Friday-evening rehearsal shortly after Mara was hired: "Only three dancers were there. She asked where the rest of the class was, and when she heard 'football' she became very agitated and said, 'I didn't leave New York for this.' However, after a short while she calmed down and declared: 'I will work with who is here.'"

Mississippi, such locations included Charlottesville, Virginia, and Miami, Florida, where the Jackson Ballet was awarded great acclaim."

The speed with which Mara built the ballet company in Mississippi was impressive indeed, but it was not without its obstacles. She recounted the challenges she faced upon arrival in Jackson:

> First, there existed a separate ballet organization called Mississippi Ballet Theatre with a separate Board, a separate Artistic Director, and separate supporters. Secondly, the Guild was a small group, not a city-wide presence as I had thought. Finally, and most importantly, there was no real audience for ballet. The parents and relatives of the children who studied in the ballet schools constituted the audiences and they were interested only in their own children. The men, in particular, had to be dragged by their wives to see the children once a year in the annual recitals, and this constituted, as far as they were concerned, the art of ballet. Every child who took lessons was called a "ballerina." The subject was tabu for boys.

Thalia Mara teaching a group of dance instructors. Photograph by John F. Mahoney. Courtesy of the estate of Thalia Mara.

Cover program of Jackson Ballet Guild, dated March 31, 1977. Courtesy of the estate of Thalia Mara.

Mara quickly discovered that she was a long way from the audiences that were stampeding into Lewisohn Stadium. It was going to be a much harder task to create public support for ballet in a city like Jackson.

However, as she continued to develop her ballet company, Mara learned much about her new city, and what she recognized changed everything. She told writer Bettye Jolly in a 1977 article for *Jackson Magazine* that she saw firsthand that Jackson was a sports town: "There was such a keen interest in sports. . . . I began searching for a way to stimulate a similar interest in ballet." The solution she came up with was as visionary as the chairman of the board of the Ballet Guild challenged her to be during her interview for the job. Mara explained, "Since the people (particularly the men who would provide the financial support) were so sports-minded, it occurred to me that the word 'competition' was something they could relate to. . . . I proposed to my Board that we bring the International Ballet Competition to Jackson. I envisioned the Competition as part of the Jackson Ballet and its support group the Guild."

The International Ballet Competition, or IBC for short, is a two-week "Olympic-style" competition for top young dancers. Just like the Olympics, competitors from across the globe vie for gold, silver, and bronze medals, as well as cash prizes and professional contracts. The first International Ballet Competition premiered in 1964. William Como, editor in chief of *Dance Magazine*, described that first-ever competition:

> Sixty-two dancers representing nineteen countries participated in the first major international ballet competition held on the Black Sea in Varna, Bulgaria. . . . The pressure was fierce. Rehearsals at Varna sometimes started at 11 P.M. after the evening's competitions. The international jury made up of outstanding artists met as early as 3:30 A.M. to discuss the announcements to be made the next morning.

Eventually this single contest grew into a cycle of ballet competitions that rotated among the three cities of Varna, Moscow, and Tokyo.[31] When

31. Mikhail Baryshnikov won the gold medal at the first Moscow competition in 1969. He was seventeen.

Mara began her inquiry about hosting it in Jackson, she was elated to learn that competition officials were, in fact, already conducting research into site locations in the United States. Mara recounted in an interview with writer Chrissy Wilson ahead of the fourth USA IBC in Jackson that she knew all the committee officials in New York that were tasked with looking for a United States city to host the competition. Members of this New York committee included Donald Saddler, Jane Hermann, William Como, Natasha Deakin, Walter Terry, and Genevieve Oswald. They were considering Philadelphia, but Mara opened their minds to the South and to Jackson:

> A lot of people on the committee were friends of mine, and I called one of the key people to say that I was already thinking about doing this, and he said they were already thinking the same thing. And I said, "Why Philadelphia—why not Jackson?" And he said, "Well, why not? Maybe Jackson is better: as a small city, it would attract more attention and it is middle America." So he came down and we talked it over and began working on it.

The "key" person that Mara called was Walter Terry, a *New York Herald-Tribune* dance critic and IBC judge. *Clarion-Ledger* reporter Virgi Lindsay shared the rest of the story:

> Terry came to Jackson to determine if the city had the facilities for an IBC. He and Mara met with Gov. Cliff Finch and his wife, Thelma. Finch had taken office just about a week earlier. . . . Thelma Finch had a meeting with businessmen in the Governor's Mansion to convince them that Jackson needed to host the IBC. . . . The businessmen asked: "Who will come?" Mara's fiery eyes sparkle as she recalled her reply. "I said the whole world will come." They believed her and pledged support.

Thalia Mara's photograph inside Jackson Ballet Guild program, March 1977. Courtesy of the estate of Thalia Mara.

As Mara struggled to land the IBC, Leanne Mahoney remembered Mara herself saying, "People thought I was crazy." One board member at the time, Mrs. J. W. Underwood, stated, "[After] the initial shock of the suggestion . . .

Les Sylphides in performance, Jackson Ballet, Jackson. Courtesy of the estate of Thalia Mara.

[we] looked at her with disbelief. . . . The competitions had never been held in the Western world and Thalia was suggesting this colossal artistic undertaking for Jackson, Mississippi, which did not even have a professional dance company at that time." Mara took a big step in proving her disbelievers wrong when, in 1977, she demonstrated what she could do when the Jackson Ballet Company performed Michel Fokine's *Les Sylphides* on March 31. It is an incredibly challenging ballet, one that the eminent critic and ballet historian Cyril W. Beaumont has described as "the most poetical of ballets of the twentieth century and, perhaps, of all time." Mara explained the ballet in the program as follows: "It is abstract in the sense that it does not follow a story line although it has a definite theme and is a visual expression of Chopin's music. The scene is a sylvan glade, the dancers represent a phantom poet and his muses at play beneath a waning moon." She then proceeded to provide critical background and explained why she chose it for her new company:

> The ballet was first danced by Vaslav Nijinsky, Anna Pavlowa,[32] Tamara Karsavina and Alexandra Baldina. It has since been interpreted by the greatest artists of the succeeding generations, including Rudolph Nureyev,[33] Mikhail Baryshnikov, Margot Fonteyn, and Natalia Makarova.
>
> In staging the work for the fledgling Jackson Ballet Company, I have in mind the development of artistic pedigree in the young dancers in

32. Anna Pavlova's last name is also often spelled as "Pavlowa."
33. Rudolf Nureyev's first name is also often spelled as "Rudolph."

Thalia Mara in *Romance*, Enrique Dorda, 1938. Dorda was one of the greatest pastel portrait painters of his time, and members of the royal family of Spain and many celebrities posed for him. *Romance* was originally choreographed in 1915 by Michel Fokine as a concert piece for Mara's former teacher, Olga Preobrajenska. In the late 1930s, Fokine staged Mara in this piece while she was a member of his ballet company. Photograph by Gil Ford. Courtesy of the estate of Thalia Mara.

Thalia Mara with Arthur Mahoney performing a jazz number at Jacob's Pillow, Becket, Massachusetts. John Lindquist Photograph. © Harvard Theatre Collection, Houghton Library, Harvard University. Courtesy of the estate of Thalia Mara.

Thalia Mara in a flamenco costume created by Italian artist/designer Marco Montedoro, head set and costume designer at Radio City Music Hall from 1932 to 1947. John Lindquist Photograph. © Harvard Theatre Collection, Houghton Library, Harvard University. Courtesy of the estate of Thalia Mara.

Arthur Mahoney and Thalia Mara in "jazz strut" on the cover of *Dance Magazine*, January 1944. Photograph taken by John Lindquist at Jacob's Pillow, Becket, Massachusetts. Courtesy of the estate of Thalia Mara.

In Jota costumes with Pepo. Courtesy of the estate of Thalia Mara.

Thalia Mara (*right*) with First Lady Jehan Sadat of Egypt at the palace in Cairo. Courtesy of the estate of Thalia Mara.

Thalia Mara in her living room in Jackson with her collection of art behind her. Courtesy of USA IBC.

Poster of fourth USA IBC, 1990. Painting by Eleanor Greaves. Courtesy of USA IBC. Photograph by Sara Berry-Lee.

Poster of fifth USA IBC, 1994. Painting by Lynn Green Root. Courtesy of USA IBC. Photograph by Sara Berry-Lee.

Thalia Mara Hall at night, Jackson. Photograph by Richard Finkelstein.

Cuban dancer José Manuel Carreño, winner of the Grand Prix City of Jackson Award of Excellence at USA IBC, 1990. Photograph by Richard Finkelstein.

Chinese dancers Wang Qifeng and Lin Jianwei at USA IBC, Jackson, 1982. Lin Jianwei defected after the competition. Courtesy of USA IBC.

Thalia Mara by artist Lynn Green Root (1954–2001). This portrait hangs in Thalia Mara Hall in Jackson. Root's style and technique have been called "exuberant" and "idiosyncratic," and she is noted for her use of strong lines and bold colors. Photograph by Roy Adkins.

> my charge; the awakening in them of love for and response to the traditions and principles to which they are heirs as I pass on to them the ideals which I imbibed from my masters.

Taking on this ambitious ballet and inviting Edward Villella and Allegra Kent, principal dancers of the New York City Ballet, to perform the major roles was a powerful statement of what Mara could accomplish. Only one year later, in 1978, after a period of negotiation, a firm offer was finally made to name Jackson the US host city for the IBC. That same year Mara represented the governor of Mississippi at the IBC in Varna, Bulgaria.

Mara had envisioned the USA IBC as part of the Jackson Ballet and its support group, the Jackson Ballet Guild; however, she did not get her wish. When legal matters were settled, a new organization was formed called Mississippi Ballet International whose sole purpose was to produce the USA IBC every four years. Robert Joffrey, renowned artistic director of the Joffrey Ballet, agreed to chair the first international panel of jurors. With the help of local, national, and international endorsements, and the energy and commitment of the citizens of Jackson, the first USA International Ballet Competition was held a year later, in June 1979, and featured seventy dancers from fifteen countries. Leanne Mahoney stated that in Mara's quest "to increase ballet audiences, she helped make Jackson one of the most ballet-savvy cities in the world."

When the first USA IBC took place in Jackson, it was an extremely exciting event. Mara told interviewer Chrissy Wilson,

> The publicity for the first IBC in 1979 was extraordinary because it was the first time. We were on the morning and evening news national network every day for about two weeks. And we had journalists here from Japan, Mexico, [and] Europe. I think public relations were much stronger the first year than in '82 or even '86 because it was the first time. People were so astounded that a small city like Jackson was holding a world event like this.

PROGRAM

I

LES SYLPHIDES

Ballet in one act

Music: Frederick Chopin *Choreography:* Michel Fokine
Staged by: Thalia Mara
Costumes: Lydia Symons *Setting:* Courtesy of Ballet West
First produced in Western Europe: Theatre du Chatelet, Paris, June 2, 1909

NOCTURNE
Katherine Thibodeaux, Marian Enochs, Beth Ware, David Keary
and
Theresa Campbell, Tracy Knight, Adele Anderson, Robin Blut, Alison Brown, Angela Clark, Shari Cochran, Denise Coker, Anna Louise Fowler, Cheryl Miller, Vonee Neel, Leah Rhemann, Cecilia Serra and Elizabeth Townsend

VALSE
Marian Enochs

MAZURKA
Katherine Thibodeaux

MAZURKA
David Keary

PRELUDE
Beth Ware

VALSE
Katherine Thibodeaux and David Keary

VALSE
Misses: Thibodeaux, Enochs, Ware, Mr. Keary and Corps de Ballet

15 MINUTE INTERMISSION

II

BALLET SUITE

Music: Dmitri Shostakovitch *Choreography:* Edward Villela
Judith Fugate Kyra Nichols
Daniel Duell Nolan T'Sani

III

Excerpts from
APOLLO, LEADER OF THE MUSES
(Apollon Musagete)

Program for presentation of *Les Sylphides*, March 1977. Courtesy of the estate of Thalia Mara.

Thalia Mara making case for USA IBC to come to Jackson. Walter Terry, member of USA IBC search committee (*seated far left*); Dale Danks, Jackson mayor (*seated center*); third gentleman, unidentified state representative (*seated far right*); Jackson, 1978. Courtesy of USA IBC.

And the people did come. Even though most people in the Jackson community were not aware of the USA IBC, tickets to the final round of competition and the awards gala sold out based on word of mouth. Patrons who saw the dancers perform in the earlier rounds spread the word in the Jackson community about the high level of competition.

Mara told Wilson in this same interview that what made Jackson stand out among IBC locations was the community support, the atmosphere surrounding the event, and the addition of the International Dance School. Mara elaborated here on the strong community involvement with the event:

> Jackson has the most community support. Jackson really turns itself out for the competition. There are about two thousand volunteers—the whole city is involved. And that's what makes it unique. There's no other competition that has host families. Every competitor who comes to Jackson has a host family. Every juror has a host family. Every member of the faculty has a host family. So they become an integrated part of the community during the two weeks that they're here. And the community becomes an integrated part of the competition. The involvement of the community is really unique. And it's one thing that the competitors and jurors and others who come here are just absolutely overwhelmed with—the hospitality and warmth. They always want to come back.

The atmosphere that Mara described came from the community and the auxiliary events surrounding the competition. Mara served as artistic director for the first five IBCs in Jackson and was responsible for developing the supplementary programming. According to the USA IBC website, for the first IBC in Jackson, an exhibition of dance-related art, entitled *Dance Image: A Tribute to Serge Diaghilev*, was organized to provide the USA IBC audience with a visual history of the ballet costume and set designs of the early twentieth century. It honored the man who John B. Henry III, coordinator of exhibitions at the Mississippi Museum of Art at the time, credited as "not [being] merely part of an era, [but creating] an era, and it follows that the achievements in the art today are the inheritance left by Diaghilev from the first quarter of this century." In the program for the exhibit, Henry acknowledged, "[No] one individual has been more responsible for innovation, creativity and inspiration in the art of ballet as we know it today. . . . How fitting it is to combine such an exhibition with the first International Ballet Competition to be hosted by the United States—a competition where artists are discovered who call upon this same creative and energetic spirit to achieve uncompromised excellence." In addition to this spectacular exhibit, a dance-film festival was held at the downtown Russell C. Davis Planetarium. The film festival showcased dance-related films such as *Junction* by Paul Taylor, *Sue's Leg* by Twyla Tharp, and *Alvin Ailey—Memories and Visions*. Mara later explained why these ancillary events were necessary:

First USA IBC exhibition cover titled "Dance Image: A Tribute to Serge Diaghilev." Courtesy of USA IBC.

> Because Jackson is a small city and because there isn't that much to see and do, as there would be in Moscow, Helsinki,[34] or Varna, we try to plan a lot of interesting events around the competition. There are lectures, exhibitions of paintings and photographs, and master classes.

All these events were held in buildings in close proximity in downtown Jackson, making them easily accessible. Mara also organized several

34. Helsinki replaced Tokyo as an IBC city in 1982.

Madame Sofia Golovkina (1915–2004) served as jury cochairperson along with Robert Joffrey at the first-ever USA IBC in 1979. She was a former ballerina with the Bolshoi Ballet, who also directed its affiliated academy, the Moscow Bolshoi Ballet School, for many years. She is remembered as a demanding teacher, with many of her students performing exceptionally well in international competitions and joining the Bolshoi Ballet upon graduation. Here she is teaching a class at the USA IBC International Dance School, Jackson, 1979. Courtesy of the estate of Thalia Mara.

"special performances," including a presentation on the history of American dance by Walter Terry—a member of the International Ballet Executive Committee who was instrumental in bringing the USA IBC to Jackson and is considered the "Dean of American Dance Critics"—and a program entitled "Conversations: An Evening with Diaghilev" hosted by Anton Dolin, the first British dancer to join Diaghilev's Ballets Russes in 1921. And, finally, Mara's third significant addition, the International Dance School, was included as a companion event to the competition, providing students and competitors with a valuable opportunity to study under the tutelage of widely recognized dance experts. All these elements combined made Jackson completely unique, and no other IBC city could compare.

Nationally known Mississippi travel writer Bern Keating covered the first USA IBC and published his reflections in *Signature Magazine*. With insight only a native Mississippian could have, Keating perceptively observed the effect the first competition had on the state: "For weeks, Mississippians were pounded with radio, television and newspaper announcements of the upcoming event. Weary and sore from years of bad press during the civil rights struggles, Mississippians began to lift their heads and beam as the importance of their competition began to register on them." He also noted the education of the fans during the two-week competition, from initially cheering and applauding wildly "for the most acrobatic performances" to recognizing the more sophisticated and subtle artistry of technique. Keating wrote that "by the time of the final night's gala performance of the medal winners, applause was still wildly exuberant, more nearly akin to the ovation for a Green Bay Packer touchdown than to the usual ballet acclaim, but the outbursts were increasingly in honor of subtlety rather than muscularity." Winners of the first USA IBC included Lubomir Kafka, Czechoslovakia (gold, senior division); Koenraad Onzia, Belgium (gold, junior division); and several American silver medalists: David McNaughton (senior division), Julian Montaner (junior division), Jessica Funt (junior division), and Deirdre Carberry (junior division). All in all, the first IBC was a rousing success!

Koenraad Onzia, junior gold medalist, Belgium; Jackson, 1979. Photograph copyright by Hubert Worley. Courtesy of USA IBC.

The IBC noted in its history that at the conclusion of the first US competition, a sanction was received from the International Dance Committee of the International Theatre Institute (ITI) of UNESCO for the USA IBC, a distinction the competition still holds today. Jackson thus officially joined the other ITI-sanctioned competitions that rotated each year among Bulgaria (Varna), Russia (Moscow), and Japan (Tokyo). Today, this prestigious, world-class event still operates under the aegis of the ITI, and the quadrennial competition alternates each year between Varna, Helsinki (which replaced Tokyo in 1982), Moscow, and Jackson.

First USA IBC senior gold medalist Lubomir Kafka, Czechoslovakia; and senior silver medalist David McNaughton, USA; Jackson, 1979. Photograph copyright by Hubert Worley. Worley was the official photographer of the IBC for the first five seasons. Courtesy of USA IBC.

Grand Prix City of Jackson Award of Excellence winners Nina Ananiashvili (USSR) and Andris Liepa (USSR), USA IBC, Jackson, 1986. Photograph by John F. Mahoney. Courtesy of USA IBC.

Chapter 5

The USA IBC and Other Projects (1979–1991)

The success of the ballet will create an audience that is knowledgeable about and receptive to all of the arts.

—Thalia Mara

In the five years Thalia Mara had given herself to build a professional dance program, she had accomplished extraordinary feats. The world took notice of what she had achieved in Jackson, and other cities and even countries came calling, asking for her advice and assistance with their own ballet programs. In 1979, she was invited by the Academia de Baile in Mexico City to serve as a consultant; in 1980 she was selected as the vice president of the jury for the

Above: "Fifth Position (with accompanying illustration): both legs are opened outward from the hips. The heel of the right foot is in front of the joint of the big toe of the left foot. The feet touch at all points and the knees are straight. The weight is evenly distributed over both feet." From *Steps in Ballet*, Thalia Mara.

Thalia Mara at the Japan International Ballet and Modern Dance competition. Courtesy of the estate of Thalia Mara.

third International Concours de Ballet in Japan; and in January 1981 she was invited to Cairo, Egypt, at the behest of the Egyptian government's Institute of Fine Arts. Enayat Azmi, director of the Ballet Institute, wanted Mara's advice. Politics had devastated Egypt's arts program; former Egyptian president Gamal Abdel Nasser's "friendliness to the Russians brought not only military aid and technicians, but also Russian teachers of ballet. [However], when a new pro-western era began under [Anwar] Sadat . . . the Russian technicians departed [and] so did the dance teachers, leaving an artistic vacuum which ha[d] yet to be filled."

The problems had not ended there. The hundred-year-old Khedivial Royal Opera House had burned down in 1971 along with all the costumes, sets, musical instruments, and curtains contained within. A decade later, Azmi turned to the West for help, and specifically to Mara, a woman she had met and befriended in 1979 at the first USA IBC and shortly thereafter reconnected with again in Japan on an international dance panel. Azmi also was quite familiar with the textbooks Mara had written on dance, as she had served as the translator of the Arabic editions. Thus, it was not surprising that Mara was the first person Azmi reached out to for help.

Immediately following the trip to Egypt, Mara wrote Azmi a letter that she called a "report," enumerating the problems she observed in Egypt and making recommendations to address them. "Dear Mme. Azmi," Mara opened, "I'm writing this report on my observations at the Ballet Academy over the past two weeks. I shall state my opinions frankly and honestly as you have requested me to do." She then proceeded to highlight the "many areas of weakness":

- The foremost problem . . . is the absence of really strong teachers for the daily classes and rehearsal coaches who are capable of developing the quality, style, musicality, and expression of the artist. . . .
- The dancers . . . appear to be lazy and they need self-discipline, burning ambition and zeal which are so much a part of our art. I believe that the dancers would respond if inspiring teachers and coaches were brought in to work with them. . . .
- I recommend dismissal for those dancers who do not show real talent, for those who do not take sufficient interest in their work, and for those who are overweight and do not slim down within a time limit. I believe a smaller but stronger group would better serve the interests of the Academy.

She also recommended instituting a "wage scale" so dancers would not need to seek supplementary income and finding some way "to heat the studios as it is difficult and dangerous to work with cold, stiff muscles." In an interview following the trip, Mara shared with writer Joan Hertzog that she thought she had made many useful suggestions. She told Hertzog that she had quickly observed that the dancers were undisciplined and that they were still trying to be "very Russian in their approach, using ideas that are really foreign to their traditions." She added, "I advised her to color their ballet with Egyptian traditions and ideas." During her trip, Mara also served as an ambassador of dance, meeting with the First Lady, Jehan Sadat, at the presidential palace. Mara advised Sadat that "an International Arts Festival be held in Cairo as a stimulus to the arts there, and Egypt's First Lady thought it sounded like a very good idea."

Shockingly, in 1981 Mara resigned her position as artistic director of the Jackson Ballet after developing the now critically acclaimed company. She did not resign by choice; a letter to Warren B. Ludlam Jr., chairman of the board of trustees of the Jackson Ballet, written on March 20, 1981, stated that she was "forced into an untenable position by the Board's action in adopting a budget, for next season, which makes no sense, whatsoever, to anyone who understands the workings of any ballet unit, large or small." Mara was angry; this letter read as a betrayal by the board of the Jackson Ballet who, as Mara wrote, met "without informing [her] or inviting [her] to be present, with the artistic director of a visiting regional ballet company to seek his advice." She continued: "Surely a remarkably rude way to treat me after achieving what everyone recognizes to be a phenomenal success for the Jackson Ballet in a singularly short period of time. And, particularly, since the whole thing was created from scratch based on my artistic ideas, principles and standards." She was furious, especially because, Mara noted, "A budget was prepared and approved by the Finance Committee without a single word to me and without any consultation whatever." This budget was then approved by the board, and she was expected to work within its framework even though she stated she found it impossible to do so. Mara reminded Ludlam in very moving language of what she had accomplished:

> Through much labor and dedication and with the great desire to create a first class ballet for Jackson and the State of Mississippi[,] I have built, over the past five years, an artistic entity which already has established a reputation nation-wide, and even internationally, due to my travels. In all my travels and contacts with organizations abroad I, as an individual, have represented what the Jackson Ballet has achieved.
>
> Now I cannot be part of a situation where I must compromise my standards, my personal reputation and the reputation of The Jackson Ballet which I have labored so hard to create.

Kathy Thibodeaux performing with Homer Garza at USA IBC, Jackson, 1982. Courtesy of USA IBC.

Despite her obvious displeasure with the board, she concluded her letter wishing that they could all remain friends, with Mara continuing to serve as artistic consultant and honorary chairman for the USA IBC. The second USA IBC was held in Jackson in 1982 and perhaps was even more exciting than the first since the city was now familiar with the competition and knowledgeable as to what to expect. And this time around the competition field was larger, with seventy-eight dancers representing nineteen countries. Among the competitors were several American dancers, including two who earned medals: Janie Parker, who was the first American to win a gold medal; and Jackson-native

Kathy Thibodeaux, senior silver medalist, USA IBC, Jackson, 1982. Her partner was Mehdi Bahiri. Photograph by John F. Mahoney. Courtesy of USA IBC.

Kathy Thibodeaux, who took home the silver medal in the senior division. Sue Lobrano, former USA IBC executive director, recalled Thibodeaux's win: "When I think back over past competitions, I remember that as a very happy moment . . . because, in a way, we felt like she belonged to all of us."

Politics also played a part in the second USA IBC in Jackson. The US Congress and former president Ronald Reagan passed a joint resolution designating Jackson as the official home of the USA IBC, which was publicly presented during the competition. And Chinese dancer Lin Jianwei used the competition as an opportunity to defect.[35] With prearranged assistance, he made his way to New Orleans for asylum and to freedom. Chinese dancers did not participate in the competition again until 1990.

Mara stayed busy in between USA IBCs conducting workshops all over the country. In 1982 she was invited by Newcomb College at Tulane University for Dance Awareness Week, where she offered classes in classical ballet; in 1983 she served on the advisory panel as well as contributed choreography for the Pacific Ballet Theater in Portland, Oregon; and in

35. A photo of Lin Jianwei with partner Wang Qifeng appears in the color insert.

Thalia Mara with USA IBC judges, 1986. Photograph copyright by Hubert Worley. Courtesy of the estate of Thalia Mara.

1983 and 1984 she was a featured instructor of a summer course for dance teachers at the Kansas City Ballet School. Then the third USA IBC came around, but it almost didn't happen. The USA IBC was faced with an overwhelming challenge at the beginning of that year: after successfully lobbying the state legislature for a $375,000 appropriations bill, the governor vetoed the appropriation. "The loss of funding was a terrific financial blow to the USA IBC," according to the history provided on the USA IBC website. Dale Danks, who served as mayor of Jackson from 1977 to 1989 during the USA IBC's most critical growth years, called an emergency meeting of the city's corporate and business leaders to raise the needed money. Danks had seen firsthand what Mara could do. He recalled in a 2001 interview with Sherry Lucas how Mara "was as calm as a cucumber" after flood damage at the auditorium threatened the very first IBC. "Her perseverance . . . inspired me and others, who had our hands full at the time, to do what we needed to have the competition, and we had it," Danks said. Danks was by Mara's side again in 1986, organizing a successful fundraising campaign that rescued the third IBC.

For the third USA IBC, Mara accepted the post of artistic director and continued to serve in that capacity for the fourth (1990) and fifth (1994) competitions as well. And during her time in this role, the competition continued to grow. In 1986 there were eighty-nine dancers from twenty-six countries represented, and for the first time two dancers from the Soviet Union competed. The couple, Andris Liepa and Nina Ananiashvili, not only competed but won the grand prize: the Grand Prix City of Jackson Award of Excellence. The competition itself was also recognized, being selected as one of the "Top Twenty Events in the Southeast" by the Southeastern Tourism Society, an honor that has been bestowed on the competition every year it has been held since 1986.

Herbert M. Simpson, who covered the 1986 competition for *Dance Magazine*, raved about the performance of the competitors and the city of Jackson. About the competition he wrote:

> Unlike last summer's International Ballet Competition in Moscow or those in Jackson in 1979 and 1982, this year's competition had no unqualified or embarrassingly coached participants to eliminate in Round I. Even the thirty-two entrants eliminated in a last-minute qualifying round looked able. At the gala awards performance, a marvelous concert, artistic values alone were emphasized. The distinguished jurors (one each from twenty countries) attempted to maintain the highest artistic standards with fairness.

Opening night of USA IBC, Jackson, 1986. Thalia Mara (*right*) with Yuri Grigorovich (*left*), USSR co-chairman of juror's panel. Courtesy of the estate of Thalia Mara.

Senior men's gold medalist Vadim Pisarev, USA IBC, Jackson, 1986. Photograph copyright by Hubert Worley. Courtesy of USA IBC.

Soviet dancers Nina Ananiashvili and Andris Liepa, winners of the Grand Prix Award, USA IBC, Jackson, 1986. Photograph copyright by Hubert Worley. Courtesy of USA IBC.

Thalia Mara teaching at the barre, Jackson, 1986. Photograph by John F. Mahoney. Courtesy of USA IBC.

Grand Prix City of Jackson Award of Excellence winners Nina Ananiashvili (USSR) and Andris Liepa (USSR), USA IBC, Jackson, 1986. Photograph by John F. Mahoney. Courtesy of USA IBC.

Thalia Mara teaching a ballet class, Jackson, June 1986. Photograph by John F. Mahoney. Courtesy of USA IBC.

And about Jackson he was extremely complementary:

> The Mississippi competition staff and its volunteers handled all the logistics smoothly. Many (including all the Russians) remarked on the friendly Southern hospitality in Jackson. Mississippi is one of the poorest states in the nation, and Jackson is a small city. That it would raise a million dollars and work to host an international ballet competition every four years is praiseworthy—and a rebuke to larger, wealthier U.S. centers less supportive of the arts.

Thalia Mara's vision always extended beyond national borders, and after being successfully involved with the USA IBC and her own international consulting work, she imagined another global event taking place in Jackson. She described it in the following document, typed on her own personal stationery:

> Having for the past nine years been engaged in cultural exchange with various nations of the world via the International Ballet Competition, and having very successfully hosted three Competitions involving some thirty-six countries (the last, in June of 1986), the City of Jackson and the

> State of Mississippi are now ready to move forward with an even more important program aimed at aiding the peace initiative by hosting an International Arts Festival for Peace. . . .
>
> Using our contacts with the many nations we already are working with, and utilizing our already existent organizations we, in Mississippi, are prepared to issue a call to all nations, Middle East, European, Far East, West, South and North to unite in a three week Festival, For All Mankind, to be held in Jackson, Mississippi, in June 1989.

This beautiful two-page statement calling for an International Arts Festival for Peace espoused Mara's sincere belief that the arts are the best and most authentic way to bring people together. She laid out her creed in several pithy statements:

> It is a known fact that the arts and the artists of all nations are bridge builders of mutual understanding between peoples and nations.
>
> Where words may fail because they arouse suspicions, or are deceitful, the arts succeed because of their inherent honesty and spiritual appeal to all mankind. . . .
>
> The arts, then, can play an important part in creating mutual understanding, for they reveal the soul of the people, cutting across the artificial differences of race, color, creed and national chauvinism with empathy; stressing, not the differences, but, the oneness of all mankind united under one God, Universal Love, no matter what His name be called.

She then issued a call for participating nations to send any type of musical, dramatic, or artistic groups that represented that country's culture or heritage, including folk-dance ensembles, ballet companies, opera groups, choral groups, theater groups, arts exhibitions, films, and the like. She also directly addressed politicians, requesting them to attend "and to be drawn into the atmosphere of cordiality, brotherhood and amicable exchanges that are certain to be present." She underpinned this personal document with the submission of a twenty-one-page, detailed proposal for the three-week festival to take place June 9 through July 1, 1989. The budget was meticulously laid out (nothing too minor was omitted) as were all events she imagined taking place, from conferences and seminars to a film series at the planetarium to blockbuster entertainment, which included names such as Liza Minnelli, Barbra Streisand, Stevie Wonder, Dolly Parton, and even the Grateful Dead! All Jackson arts organizations were slated to be involved—the Mississippi Museum of Art, Jackson

Opera, New Stage Theatre, Ballet Mississippi—and were included in the proposal. Perhaps the most interesting section of the entire document was the conclusion, as Mara and coauthor Alfred Stern quoted Harvard professor of theology Harvey Cox as well as Albert Einstein:

> Our links to yesterday and tomorrow depend on the aesthetics, emotional and symbolic aspects of human life—on saga, play and celebration. When a civilization becomes alienated from its past and cynical about its future, its spiritual energy flags. It stumbles and declines. "*Without festivity and fantasy, man would not really be an historical being at all.*"
>
> The Festival's thematic concept of For All Humanity—World Peace to be nourished by free and shared cultural exchange is also validated by Albert Einstein who wrote: "Peace cannot be kept by force. It can only be achieved by understanding."

Sadly, this incredible event, which Mara injected with such passion and purpose, would not happen. She would fail to raise the required sums. However, Mara was not easily thwarted and would plan equally large-scale events in the near future.

But before that would happen, Mara had another honor to receive and USA IBC to organize, set to be held from June 17 to July 1, 1990. In March 1990, Mara, alongside literary giant Eudora Welty, was honored by Mississippi governor Ray Mabus at the Governor's Awards for Excellence in the Arts. Welty was granted the highest honor, the Lifetime Achievement Award, but Mara was given a singular honor as well, the Mississippi Artist's Achievement Award. Although Mara was recognized worldwide for her contributions to dance, this award was the first she received in Mississippi. She stated that she was "very touched and deeply moved" by the honor, but said it "reflect[ed] the success of the IBC," which she credited to "many, many people in Mississippi and in Jackson who ha[d] worked hard. There [we]re many unsung heroes."

In June, for the fourth IBC, Mara had made an individual financial contribution that illustrated beyond question her unwavering commitment to the competition. She donated $65,000, funds she had earned from her former school, the National Academy of Ballet and Theatre Arts. As a stipulation of the gift, Mara insisted that "this money [wa]s to be spent solely for operating expenses between October 1, 1988 and September 30, 1990." Sue Lobrano, executive director of the USA IBC at the time, wrote to Mara in her thank-you letter: "As founder of this unique event, we are grateful to you in so many different ways. Personally, I want you to know how much I appreciate your support." She also included a contract for Mara to sign requesting her services as artistic director.

The fourth USA IBC was the biggest one yet, with 109 dancers representing twenty-six countries. It was dedicated to Robert Joffrey, founder of the Joffrey Ballet, friend of Thalia Mara's, and jury chairman of the USA IBC since its inception, who had died in March 1988. To honor Joffrey, his company performed at the opening ceremony. Edward Stierle, a Joffrey dancer and 1986 USA IBC gold medalist, choreographed "Lachrymosa" and dedicated it to Joffrey's memory. The fourth USA IBC also was noteworthy for having the first Cuban dancer, José Manuel Carreño, compete and win the Grand Prix City of Jackson Award of Excellence. Carreño was sensational; IBC executive director Sue Lobrano recalled, "The whole audience came unglued . . . [and] Thalia Mara [stated], 'He had everyone out of their seats. He was absolutely spectacular.'" (See photo in color insert.) The USA IBC also featured, as an auxiliary arts program, the ballet-competition photographs of John F. Mahoney. Mahoney had covered nine international ballet competitions in all four host cities: Moscow (thrice), Varna (thrice), Jackson (twice), and Helsinki (once). Mahoney came to Jackson for the opening of the exhibition. He was one of only a few Americans (including competitors) present at the

Robert Joffrey, jury chairman or co-chairman of first three USA IBCs. Photograph by Ruth D. Levy. Courtesy of the estate of Thalia Mara.

Thalia Mara speaking about fourth USA IBC, Jackson, April 1989. Photograph by John F. Mahoney. Courtesy of USA IBC.

1981 IBC in Moscow (where American Amanda McKerrow won gold that year), so his photographs are significant for capturing the history of the competition during its earliest years. He wrote Mara in a letter after the exhibition that he "was honored to be asked to display [his] work." Finally, the 1990 IBC was special for launching the tradition of naming a Mississippi artist as the official artist of the competition. This artist is tasked with creating a commemorative poster. In 1990 the artist named was Eleanor Godfrey Greaves, and her poster (see color insert) featured a still life of ballet costumes collected over the years by Mara and her husband, Arthur Mahoney.[36] Other Mississippi artists named as USA IBC artists since 1990 include Lynn Green Root, William Baggett, Kennith Humphrey, P. Sanders McNeal, Brent Funderburk, Andrew Bucci, and Kit Fields.

36. Mahoney and Mara never divorced. He would return regularly from California to Jackson to visit Mara, and, after a fifteen-year separation, he returned to Jackson permanently. He died at Mara's home in Jackson in 1985 at the age of eighty-one.

Two people who thought the 1990 competition was an especially resounding success were Ben Stevenson and Arnold Spohr. Both men should know, as Stevenson garnered the USA IBC Choreography Award and Spohr was a Canadian dancer, choreographer, and recently retired artistic director of the Royal Winnipeg Ballet. They sent Mara separate thank-you notes following the competition, complimenting her on the professionalism of the event, the level of competition, and the success of Jackson as the USA IBC's home. Stevenson wrote:

> Dear Thalia,
>
> I have been meaning to write to you ever since we returned from the Competition to tell you how thoroughly professional every aspect of the Competition was handled. They should have given you a gold medal for your tireless efforts and the support you and your entire staff provided.
>
> . . . Personally I thought the competition was tougher this year than in previous years which certainly indicates how serious this competition has become and will continue to be under your leadership. . . .
>
> Sincerely,
> Ben Stevenson

Similarly, Spohr wrote the following to thank Mara:

> Dear Thalia Mara,
>
> Thank you for an exciting, stimulating, competition. You have done wonders with establishing Jackson, Miss., as a glowing beacon for international dance with the competition. Your legacy for the community and dancers everywhere has certainly been established. You have enriched so many lives and left . . . Jackson a shining symbol for dance.
>
> With admiration and respect,
> Love,
> Arnold (Spohr)

Thalia Mara sat down for an interview with Chrissy Wilson on the eve of the fourth IBC and looked back on its past history and success. When she was asked at the conclusion of the interview if she thought the USA IBC as an event could grow even more, she responded, "How could it grow? We already have the top dancers from all over the world. First, there are not that many great dancers; it has to be very selective, and we have to keep the standards high." However, what she did hope would continue was support for all the arts in the city:

> Dance is not an independent art: it involves music; it involves design; it involves drama; it involves all of these things. When people see dance, they are also seeing the contributions of the artists who designed the costumes, who light the stage. So I would like to see all of the arts in Jackson really understanding that they contribute to each other. The success of one does not diminish the other. If you go to the ballet and like the experience, you're going to become more interested in symphonic music. And you're going to become more interested in theatre. It's not necessary for anyone in Jackson to feel left out, to feel that if dance is going forward that their art is not. On the contrary, I am sure that the success of the ballet that I came here and organized was directly influential in the growth of the symphony orchestra. It augmented itself; it became more successful. Cooperation among the arts is very important. . . . The success of the ballet will create an audience that is knowledgeable about and receptive to all of the arts.

This statement proved prophetic, as Mara's next projects included more than just ballet.

At the 2002 USA IBC, Thalia Mara (*center*) was presented with a Lifetime Achievement Award and a gold medal for her long career in the arts. Courtesy of the estate of Thalia Mara.

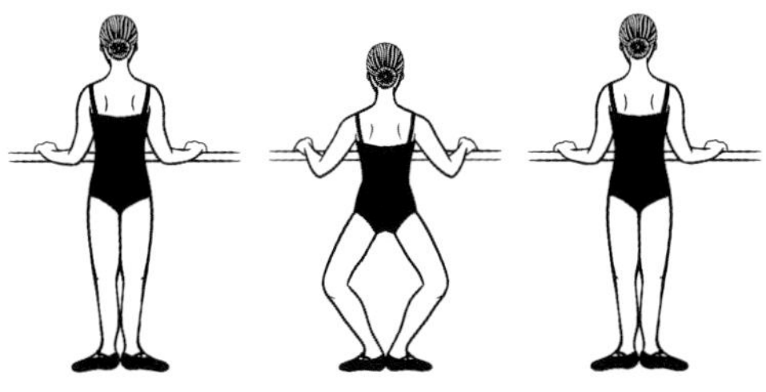

Chapter 6

The Thalia Mara Arts International Foundation (1991–1998)

I wish somebody would say, "Here, Thalia. Here's a couple million, start the thing."

—Thalia Mara

Thalia Mara's gifts to her adopted city and state were not limited to the USA IBC. Even though her vision for an International Arts Festival for Peace was not realized, the planning she did was not for naught. Similar planning went into another venture that did, in fact, succeed: establishing the Thalia Mara Arts International Foundation in 1991, a 501(c)(3) tax-exempt organization whose mission statement read as follows:

Above: "The *Demi-Plié*: Your very first exercise at the barre is the *demi-plié*. It is most important for you to master this and later the *grand plié*, because the *plié* is the basis of everything you do in ballet." From *Steps in Ballet*, Thalia Mara.

Flyer of Thalia Mara Arts International Foundation. Courtesy of the estate of Thalia Mara.

The mission of the Thalia Mara Arts International Foundation is to preserve, nurture, and advance the education, understanding, and love of the arts in all their manifestations, and in particular, to promote the importance of classical arts in education as a vehicle for integrating fundamental ideals and values of integrity and morality into present day society.

The Thalia Mara Arts International Foundation believes that the arts—performing, visual and design, film and media, literary and language—are of vital importance to the future of civilization. They tell the story of our history, and light the way into our future. Our children are that future. The arts are the vehicle for embracing the future and ours to create a better way for them.

In addition to the mission statement, Mara laid out seven principal goals that the foundation hoped to achieve:

1. Sponsor and support the Yamaha International Junior Original Concert in Jackson.
2. Sponsor the Second Salon International Visual Arts Competition.
3. Develop public/private arts education partnerships.
4. Present special programs and projects in the arts.
5. Create a professional education theatre in Mississippi working with education programs of the schools both public and private.
6. Establish a regional costume rental house.
7. Create an arts reference library.

To fulfill its mission and goals, the foundation was able to provide funds for a broad range of professional arts activities enumerated above, such as the creation and support of an international arts library; the creation and support of a professional children's theater in Mississippi; the establishment of a regional costume-rental house; and the provision of grants primarily directed to artists and arts endeavors in Mississippi.

As with the Jackson Ballet, it did not take long for the foundation with Mara at the helm to leave its mark on the city. In 1992, one year after the foundation was established, Mara was appointed by Governor Kirk Fordice to spearhead the Mississippi Homecoming Celebration, recognizing 175 years of Mississippi statehood. Another noteworthy foundation project included providing scholarships for teachers training at the USA IBC's dance school. The 1994 USA IBC was another magnificent event for the city of Jackson with Mara as artistic director and the International Dance School she founded "filled to capacity, with more than 300 students from 26 states and five countries participating." Hillary Rodham Clinton served as honorary chair of the competition, and the Mississippi Museum of Art

Marina Antonova and Igor Antonova, who were individual winners in the senior division, partnered to win best couple medalist at the 1994 USA IBC, Jackson. Courtesy of USA IBC.

hosted a Degas exhibit featuring seventy-four bronze sculptures as well as paintings, pastels, and drawings by the artist. The 1994 competition also received a Regional Designation Award in the Arts from the Atlanta Committee for the Olympic Games and was selected as Event of the Year by the Arts Alliance of Jackson and Hinds County.

It was also during the fifth USA IBC Awards Gala that Mara herself was honored for her contributions to dance. On June 28, 1994, at the Mississippi Museum of Art, Mara received the Circle of Dance Award for Lifetime Contributions to Dance Education. The Circle of Dance Award was sponsored by *Dance Teacher Now* magazine and had only been awarded twice since 1989. A description of the award stated, "It commemorates those efforts in dance which are both timely and timeless, growing and permanent—the torch which is passed from hand to hand." The publisher of *Dance Teacher Now* was present for the ceremony, and she honored Mara and the USA IBC for its "continuing emphasis on education, [which] includes the International Dance School, in which competitors and other young dancers have the opportunity to take classes alongside their peers with master teachers from around the world." The presentation of a portrait of Mara by Mississippi artist Lynn Green Root, who was the IBC poster artist that year, was a highlight of the ceremony (see color insert). Today the portrait hangs in the home of the IBC, Thalia Mara Hall, which was originally known as the Jackson Municipal Auditorium but was renamed for Mara that same year, 1994.

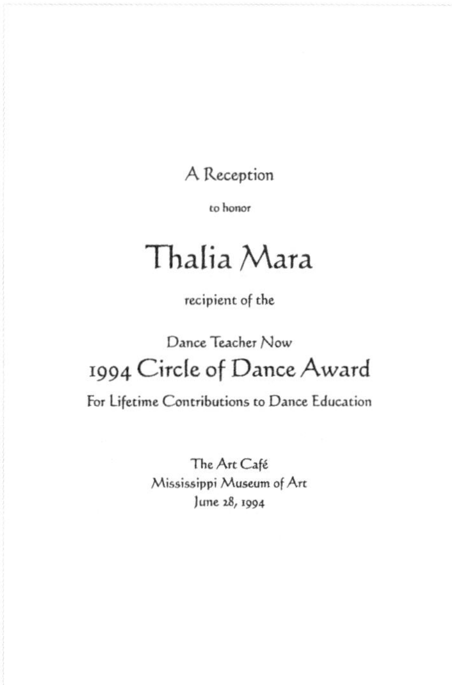
A Reception

to honor

Thalia Mara

recipient of the

Dance Teacher Now

1994 Circle of Dance Award

For Lifetime Contributions to Dance Education

The Art Café
Mississippi Museum of Art
June 28, 1994

1994 Circle of Dance Award program. Courtesy of USA IBC.

The renaming of the 2,430-seat auditorium to Thalia Mara Hall was an honor for which Mara had no words. "I am rather overwhelmed," she told the council after the vote. "It is a very humbling experience to have people say the nice things that have been said about me and to receive the kind of outcrying of love that has been given to me in the last four years." Two councilwomen, Marcia Weaver of Ward 6 and Margaret Barrett of Ward 7, led the

Thalia Mara (*fourth from left*), standing in front of Thalia Mara Hall, Jackson. Courtesy of the estate of Thalia Mara.

effort to recognize Mara in this way. Barrett said that it was "through the efforts of Thalia Mara [that] the doors of our city were opened to the world and people have come to see what Jackson, Mississippi, has to offer."

During the 1990s, Thalia Mara's work at the foundation expanded beyond the USA IBC. In 1997, the foundation, along with the Yamaha Corporation of America and the Yamaha Music Foundation of Japan, sponsored and brought to Jackson the Yamaha International Junior Piano Competition and Concert, which featured ten winners, ages nine through eighteen, whose original music compositions were chosen out of three hundred submitted. In 1998, Mara also organized and financed S'il Vous Plait et Merci, a French course for children held in libraries around the city. Another proposal she wrote during this period was for a pilot school to test a curriculum integrating the arts and humanities with the current academic curriculum in the city. In this proposal, Mara described at length her experience founding the National Academy of Ballet and Theatre Arts in 1963 in New York City, citing it as a very "successful operation." She wrote that "poor students became good students as their interests were piqued and developed" and that "upon graduation . . . students who elected to go on to college to further their education were eminently prepared to do so." She expected the same results for her new school project and was extremely detailed in her planning and thinking, as she had been in other proposals. For example, for first grade she envisioned the following:

> Get humanities scholars to come to talk and act out events. Let the children act out situations and ideas which they write themselves. Make a field trip to Philadelphia to visit the Choctaw reservation. Have some Indian children visit the school and spend a day with students. Learn the beliefs of the Indians, their music, dance, their costumes. Prepare an Indian meal. Learn the history of corn. See their artwork from the past.
>
> Have some Spanish (Mexican) children bring food, learn the Jota (the national dance of Spain), get a Spanish guitarist, a bagpipe player to come, learn their songs. Ditto the French and English.

She did the same type of curriculum planning for second and third grade as well, in addition to including a detailed budget for the first three years the program was in place (1994–95, 1995–96, 1996–97). Mara successfully implemented this program at Madison Station Elementary School, expanding its art program. Teacher Elizabeth Gober stated in an interview with Sherry Lucas, "The school is meshing the curriculum Mara developed for her ballet and theatre academy in New York, with what was already in progress as its part in the Mississippi Arts Commission's Whole Schools Initiative. . . . The school's five-year goal is to have full-time, long-term specialists in visual arts, drama and dance as well as music."

The sixth USA IBC in 1998 was another blockbuster event for the city, generating $4,563,000. Bruce Weber, a reporter who covered the sixth IBC for the *New York Times*, acknowledged this when he wrote, "At a time when international [dance] competitions are proliferating around the

Senior gold medalist Rasta Thomas (USA), USA IBC, Jackson, 1998. Courtesy of USA IBC.

Eudora Welty, Thalia Mara, and Margaret Walker Alexander at the Mayor's Arts Achievement Honors, Jackson, 1998. Photograph by Kay Holloway. Courtesy of the estate of Thalia Mara.

world—there are now about 15 of them. . . . Jackson's, astonishingly enough, may well be the best attended, most fiercely contested of them all." The sixth USA IBC included eighty-seven dancers from twenty-six countries competing for $60,000 in prize money and scholarships. But, perhaps more significantly, it ushered in what writer Sherry Lucas described as a "banner season" of art events for the city of Jackson, many of which involved Mara or her foundation. In addition to the sixth USA IBC, the spectacular *Splendors of Versailles* exhibition opened at the Mississippi Museum of Art, and another noteworthy event occurred on a single night in July. On July 30, 1998, Mara was honored, along with Eudora Welty and Margaret Walker Alexander, at the Mayor's Arts Achievement Honors. All were recognized for their artistic contributions to the city and the state. The three were celebrated at an event entitled "Three Women . . . Three Lifetimes . . . One Night" for their extraordinary achievements in the arts: Welty and Walker for literature and Mara for dance and dance education.

Thalia Mara was also commended by the Mississippi legislature in 1998 in Senate Concurrent Resolution 649 for "a lifetime of achievement in dance and her contributions to education and the influence of the arts on education." This official resolution, which listed all the major milestones of Mara's career and contributions to the city of Jackson and beyond, stated the following in the conclusion:

> WHEREAS, the Capital City and the State of Mississippi have reaped untold benefit and prestige from the tireless efforts of this one woman who, while not a native daughter, has remained to live, work and promote the arts here to the everlasting advantage of all Mississippians, who are proud and gratified to be able to call her one of our own by her choice if not by birth:
>
> NOW, THEREFORE, BE IT RESOLVED BY THE MISSISSIPPI STATE SENATE, THE HOUSE OF REPRESENTATIVES CONCURRING THEREIN, that we do hereby commend Miss Thalia Mara for her monumental contributions to education and the arts in Mississippi, for her role in the development of dance not just in Mississippi, but worldwide, and for her enrichment and revitalization of the entire cultural community of Mississippi.

But even as Mara was being honored by the Mississippi legislature for a lifetime of work, she was not done yet. At age eighty-eight, this "petite powerhouse" was still organizing magnificent programs for her adopted state. In 1999 the Thalia Mara Arts International Foundation launched the World Performance Series, with the objective of bringing performances and related educational programs to Mississippi that exposed its citizens to the epitome of art. The initial phase began in early 1999. Mara put the board together and asked Lawrence and Jan Farrington to serve as chairmen of the Founders Circle and initiate fundraising. Full-time staff included Robert Canon as executive director, Dawn Buck as operations manager, and Carla S. Wall as development director. Wall remembered that everyone went to work with Mara's directive foremost in mind: "Sell out the first performance." And that is exactly what they did.

When Mara announced the first six performances of the series at a news conference, representatives of the city were incredibly excited. On the schedule was the American Ballet Theatre performing *Don Quixote* and featuring 1990 USA IBC Grand Prix winner José Manuel Carreño; the Aquila Theatre of London performing *King Lear*; Joshua Bell, virtuoso violinist in recital; the Alvin Ailey American Dance Theater, a world-renowned contemporary dance company comprised of Black dancers; Cirque Éloize, a theatrical French circus from Canada; and the Lincoln

Center Jazz Orchestra with trumpeter Wynton Marsalis. Jackson mayor Harvey Johnson Jr. stated at the time of the announcement, "This [series] will open the door for other quality events to be held in Jackson," and Jack Kyle, executive director of the Mississippi Commission for Cultural Exchange, said, "I'm very excited to see an organization in Jackson focus on presenting world class performing arts. . . . For too long we have been off the circuit of exposure."

All of these artists' visits featured an educational component, too. The American Ballet Theatre offered two master classes at Belhaven College; the Aquila Theatre of London gave a special matinée performance for approximately five hundred middle-school students and the director conducted a two-hour class at New Stage Theatre for aspiring actors; and Joshua Bell met with members of the string section of the Mississippi Youth Orchestra and displayed, performed, and discussed differences in tone of his two Stradivarii.[37] Members of the three other performing groups also integrated themselves into the community: two Alvin Ailey dancers gave a talk at the Alamo Theatre; performers with Cirque Éloize visited Jackson's APAC School to work with dance and drama students; and Wynton Marsalis visited a class at Jackson State University. Wall stated that Mara's commitment to arts education was present in all of her plans and programs: "One of my responsibilities was to develop meaningful, interactive educational programs for the World Performance Series where students had the opportunity to not only see but interact with the performers. The World Performance Series brought together two of

The
Mayor's Arts
Achievement
Honors

In Tribute To

Thalia Mara
Margaret Walker Alexander
Eudora Welty

Thursday, July 30, 1998

6:30 to 8:00 pm

Thalia Mara Hall

Jackson, Mississippi

Program for Mayor's Arts Achievement Honors, Jackson, July 30, 1998. Courtesy of the estate of Thalia Mara.

37. Stradivarii are considered the most famous violins in the world. They were made by master craftsman Antonio Stradivari of Cremona, Italy, in the seventeenth and early eighteenth centuries.

World Performance Series program, 1999. Courtesy of the estate of Thalia Mara.

Thalia's lifelong passions—excellence in performance and arts education. She believed they could be life changing."

In 2001, two years before her death at age ninety-two, Mara was still engaged in multiple projects and envisioning new ideas. For the World Performance Series that year, Mara's theme was Spanish to complement *The Majesty of Spain* exhibit set to open at the Mississippi Arts Pavilion in March. That exhibit, along with all related programs and cultural exhibits,

World Performance Series program, 2001. Courtesy of the estate of Thalia Mara.

was a huge success and financial boon for the city of Jackson.[38] Mara remained president of the foundation, but this time around her niece, Leanne Mahoney, led the planning and organizational efforts. The foundation invited Alicia de Larrocha, world-renowned Spanish pianist, and Teatro Flamenco, a company of Spanish dancers, guitarists, and singers

38. See "Royal Splendor in the Deep South" (June 3, 2001) by *New York Times* writer Jennifer Moses on the background and excitement this exhibit generated in Jackson.

At the 2002 USA IBC, Thalia Mara (*center*) was presented with a Lifetime Achievement Award and a gold medal for her long career in the arts. Courtesy of the estate of Thalia Mara.

led by flamenco star Maria Benitez, to participate. Perhaps not as well known to Jackson audiences, flamenco, according to Mara, would make an impression on younger audiences with its powerful percussive element and rhythm. "'I think the young kids will really be blown away. . . . If they [aren't], something's wrong with them,' she sa[id], laughing," in an interview with Sherry Lucas in 2001. Mara's plans did not end there. In the same interview she jokingly remarked, "I wish somebody would say, 'Here, Thalia. Here's a couple million, start the thing.'" That thing was "a working, ultimately self-sufficient farm, run by people who [needed] a second chance in life, with space, too, for homeless animals."[39] She also dreamed of founding a museum and dance archive. Sadly, these dreams did not materialize, but they do speak to her boundless energy and endless storehouse of ideas.

Perhaps the most meaningful recognition Thalia Mara received came in 2002 at the final USA IBC she would ever attend. It was at the seventh competition that a gold medal was presented to Thalia Mara herself, not only for her dedication to the USA IBC but "for her long career in the arts."

39. Thalia Mara always loved animals. She had her pet parrot for almost fifty years and many, many cats.

Edward Villella served as honorary chairman of the 2002 USA IBC, and he presided over an "emotional ceremony [that] paid homage to the founder of the USA IBC, surrounding her with colleagues, friends, and hundreds of red roses." The USA IBC itself was also honored for being named Event of the Year by the Metro Jackson Visitor Industry Council, receiving the Governor's Award for Excellence in the Arts, and being chosen as one of the Top 100 Events in North America by the American Bus Association.

Despite all her honors and awards, Mara was not ready to slow down. She kept working on her various projects and plans until the final month of her life, which would come just one year later.

Thalia Mara with her niece, Leanne Mahoney.
Courtesy of the estate of Thalia Mara.

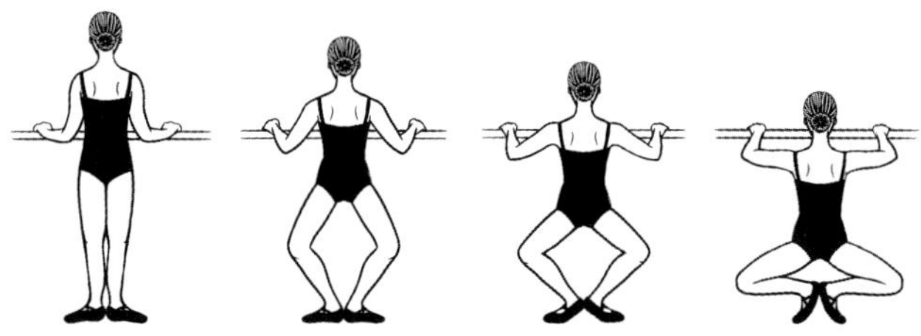

Chapter 7

Thalia Mara's Death and Legacy

My great desire as a teacher has always been to pass along the torch. I had magnificent teachers. They represented the tradition of the great Russian School and worked very hard and with a great deal of love to pass the torch to me. I have always tried to pass it to my students.

—Thalia Mara

In the fall of 2003, at the age of ninety-two, Thalia Mara suffered a series of strokes and, on October 8, died at St. Dominic Memorial Hospital in Jackson. The condolences came pouring in from all over the world:

From Takashi Iijima, former student; Nagano, Japan:

I was deeply shocked to learn of Thalia's death, though I knew her age. I am too broken-hearted to write a few lines. Mme. Thalia Mara is one of my respected teachers. . . . I learned many things from her and I loved her.

Above: "The *Grand Plié*: Do not practice the *grand plié* until your teacher tells you that you do a good *demi-plié* and may now begin learning the *grand plié*. This is very important because if you cannot hold all the proper body placement in the *demi-plié* you will never be able to do the *grand plié*." From *Steps in Ballet*, Thalia Mara.

From Gayle Miller, former director of external affairs, Capezio Ballet Makers Inc.; New York, New York:

> Capezio is saddened by the death of Thalia Mara, visionary of Jackson's first USA International Ballet Competition in 1979. Dance educator, performer, and author, she worked tirelessly to secure Jackson's distinct place in the world of dance.

From Marcus Alford, dancer, teacher, choreographer; Atlanta, Georgia:

> I'm so sorry to hear about the passing of Thalia. She was truly a great person and a ray of bright light in this Dance world. She will truly be missed.

From Glenda Brown, former artistic director, Allegro Ballet of Houston; Houston, Texas:

> I am so sorry to hear of Thalia Mara's death. She was quite an inspiration to so many in the dance world. It was Thalia's idea to incorporate Regional Dance America into the IBC program, bridging the professional, nonprofessional and student dancers together. It was a perfect marriage for RDA and . . . IBC.

From Dennis Nahat, former artistic director, Ballet San Jose; San Jose, California:

> We will miss her. . . . She was a great lady of the theater. We are all indebted to her.

In a tribute that appeared two days later in the *Clarion-Ledger*, Mara was remembered by many Mississippians. Governor Ronnie Musgrove called her "one of the state's most noble citizens . . . and we should all be grateful that she happened our way." Sue Lobrano, former executive director of the USA IBC, said, "She was small but mighty. . . . 'No' wasn't in her vocabulary, and she didn't want it to be in yours either." Lobrano also recounted Mara coming to her with "wonderful, creative ideas for the IBC" and she would respond, "'But, Thalia, that's not in our budget. We just don't have the money.' Mara's reply was 'Well, I suppose you'll just have to *find* the money.' That was the end of the subject." And David Keary, artistic director of Ballet Mississippi and former student of Mara's, described Mara's style in the studio as "driven, passionate, determined," but at home she was very

Cartoonist Marshall Ramsey's tribute to Thalia Mara, which appeared in the *Clarion-Ledger* on October 10, 2003. © Marshall Ramsey—USA TODAY NETWORK.

different. Mae Nooe, a friend, concurred, describing how she loved to cook "fine meals" for friends: "She cooked everything from scratch, no matter how elaborate . . . [but] it wasn't just the food. It was the love and sincere zest she had for sharing this with her guests."

Thalia Mara was honored by being laid in state at Thalia Mara Hall on the day before her funeral. According to Carla Wall, close friend of Mara's and principal planner of the memorial service,

> Thalia believed the arts belonged to everyone. Her work in the Jackson community was always inclusive and collaborative, so it seemed appropriate that her visitation should be in Thalia Mara Hall in downtown Jackson. I secured permission to use the hall and honor guards, and worked with the city on planned arrangements. People from all over the area came to pay their respects. The line was continuous during the afternoon. I like to think that Thalia would have been pleased to know that the community she had come to love held her in such high regard. It was her last time "on stage" but her legacy remains.

The funeral was held the day after the visitation on Saturday, October 11, at St. Andrew's Episcopal Cathedral in downtown Jackson. The

Program for "A Celebration of Life" for Thalia Mara. Cover art by P. Sanders McNeal, Mara's close friend. Courtesy of the estate of Thalia Mara.

program for this celebration of Mara's life was illustrated by her dear friend and former USA IBC artist P. Sanders McNeal with a graphite-on-paper drawing entitled *Dancer at Rest.* Pallbearers included former Jackson mayors Dale Danks and Harvey Johnson Jr., as well as USA IBC benefactor and board chair William Mounger. Mara was not Episcopalian; she was a Christian Scientist and active member of the First Church of Christ Scientist in Jackson. The funeral was held at the cathedral to accommodate all the guests. Jackson State music professor Ellistine Perkins Holly, Mara's friend and fellow Christian Scientist, often would perform during First Church of Christ Scientist services and told a reporter in a 2001 interview that Mara was upset if she was not singing on Sundays: "She would get quite disturbed and disappointed if I wasn't singing. It mattered to her. It made a difference to her. And that's one of the greatest things to Thalia. It does make a difference to her. It matters when she sees a talent that's not being used."

In the eulogy given at the funeral this idea of Mara's passion for excellence was elucidated upon. The Very Reverend Joseph O. Robinson officiated and spoke directly to this point:

> There was only one thing that Thalia could not and would not tolerate and that was mediocrity. Everything about Thalia was excellent; whether it was bringing the best talents in the world to share with her adopted city, or preparing one of her fabulous dinner parties for a small group of friends . . . Thalia knew of the difficulty in creating and achieving excellence and, for her, this was a valuable part of the process. She understood and taught us the value of hard work, discipline and dedication.

Thalia Mara's casket carried by pallbearers to a waiting hearse after services at St. Andrew's Episcopal Cathedral, Jackson, October 12, 2003. *Front right*, Jackson mayor Harvey Johnson Jr. © Vickie D. King—USA TODAY NETWORK.

That Thalia Mara cared, that it "made a difference to her," is definitely one of her legacies and is evident in the eleven books she wrote about dance, the first published in 1955, coinciding with her early years of teaching. The majority of her books are instructional texts on ballet: *First Steps in Ballet: Basic Exercises at the Barre*; *Second Steps in Ballet: Basic Center Exercises*; *Third Steps in Ballet: Basic Allegro Steps*; *Fourth Steps in Ballet: On Your Toes*; *So You Want to Be a Ballet Dancer*; *The Language of Ballet: An Informal Dictionary*;[40] *Do's and Don'ts of Basic Ballet Barre Work*; *Do's and Don'ts of Basic Center Practice Work*; *Do's and Don'ts of Basic Allegro Work*; and *Ballet: Home Practice for Beginners*. Her books received outstanding reviews from newspapers all over the country: Regina J. Woody wrote in the *New York Times* that in *On Your Toes* "Miss Mara's instructions on fitting toe shoes is worth the price of the book many times over"; the *News Journal* of Pensacola, Florida, declares of *Third Steps in Ballet* that "future ballerinas will learn much from this simple and lucid book"; and Lee Wyndham writes for the *Daily Record* of Morristown, New Jersey, that the book *Second Steps in Ballet* is "a masterpiece of simplicity; like the first book, this one, too, will be acclaimed by critics, teachers and students." After her years of performing were over and she turned to teaching, Mara's

40. Later reprints dropped the use of "informal" in the title: *The Language of Ballet: A Dictionary*.

passion, her mission, was to continue to maintain the highest standard of dance that she could for *all*—not just her students. In 2004, Richard Philp, editor in chief emeritus of *Dance Magazine*, wrote a remembrance of Mara in the October edition, stating as much:

> As a teacher, her passionate ideas about dance are spelled out in her eleven books. *Steps in Ballet* (Princeton Book Company, 2004), a new edition, combines three books by Mara into one volume. It is intended as an aid for students in practicing at home and includes a foreword to parents about choosing a teacher. In a day when those who were training dancers were not as knowledgeable as they are now, she was a fierce advocate for raising standards of instruction. She studied and performed with the leading teachers and dancers of her time: Adolph Bolm, Olga Preobrajenska, Nicholas Legat, Kurt Joos, and Michel Fokine. She married her dancing partner, Arthur Mahoney, and together they founded the National Academy of Ballet [and Theatre] Arts in New York in 1962. At that time, she felt contemporary ballet had declined into "sharp, cold movement," and she emphasized a return to "lyricism, romanticism, classicism, and musicality . . . [in which] the expressiveness of the individual must be encouraged."

In the foreword that Philp refers to, Mara wrote directly to parents about the importance of finding a competent teacher because a child's body could be irreparably injured if an instructor is not versed in anatomy:

> The bones of a young child are soft and malleable. The tendons and muscles of the feet and legs interlace with those of the back and it is the correct use of these tendons and muscles pulling against each other which build the strength and shapeliness of the ballet dancer. A good teacher knows all of these things and how to balance the exercises to develop the results of grace, beauty, and poise. Incorrect repetition of the details of these same exercises can have a disastrous effect on the feet, back, and muscular development of the legs.

Her directions to parents were quite explicit: The teacher should have had "at least four or five years of intensive instruction"; children should not begin the study of ballet until the age of eight ("there have been a few notable exceptions to this rule, but such exceptions are very rare"); the best teachers are knowledgeable in the "three distinct schools of technique in ballet: the Russian, the Italian, . . . and the French and may base [their]

Thalia Mara's instructional books. Photograph by Imani Khayyam.

system entirely on the theory of one school or on a combination of them"; and beware "the teacher to whom 'ballet' means only toe dancing . . . [as] its study should not be begun until after at least two or three years of consistent study and practice in the basic exercises of ballet." Mara also included a section dedicated to "Boys in Ballet," recognizing that the illustrations in her books are feminine, but reminding parents that ballet "began as a masculine art and it is still a manly and fine art for boys." Remembering her husband's painful experience breaking into dance without family support may explain the passionate outburst that she included in this section of the foreword:

> Many coaches are sending their basketball and football team members to ballet classes to learn coordination. Famous boxers have studied ballet to improve their footwork. It is time American boys and their parents overcome this silly attitude. . . . If you would like your son to develop a strong, healthy body, good physical and mental coordination, an appreciation of music, painting, literature, and drama—send him to a ballet class!

Mara was first and foremost a teacher. In an interview with *Belhaven College* (now Belhaven University) magazine, she said, "My great desire

Cover of Thalia Mara's *To Dance, to Live,* with drawings by Tina Mackler. Photograph by Imani Khayyam.

as a teacher has always been to pass along the torch. I had magnificent teachers. They represented the tradition of the great Russian School and worked very hard and with a great deal of love to pass the torch to me. I have always tried to pass it to my students."

In addition to her instructional texts, Mara collaborated on two books with celebrated dance illustrator Tina Mackler. The first, *The Language of Ballet: A Dictionary*, addressed "the great need," she wrote in the foreword, "for the standardization of ballet terminology in order that teaching ideas may be more easily transmitted from teacher to student and, even more importantly, that such ideas may flow more freely between teachers of differing schools and countries." Mara was always seeing the big picture and trying to eliminate confusion. She observed in this foreword that "it is not unheard of that intense arguments develop between dancers over the name of a step or the correctness of a term" due to dance instructors with little knowledge of French.

The other, *To Dance, to Live*, published in 1977, was titled after what former National Academy of Ballet and Theatre Arts student and professional dancer April Berry calls Mara's mantra. And the book lives up to that statement, as it is not about her but is a celebration of dance, with text by Mara accompanying drawings by Mackler of twenty contemporary dancers and six dance companies, including (among others) Natalia Makarova, Mikhail Baryshnikov, Margot Fonteyn, Rudolf Nureyev, Edward Villella, Judith Jamison, Martha Graham, the Joffrey Ballet, Dancers of Bali, and Ballet Folklórico de México. Mara's niece, Leanne Mahoney, stated of the book, "Mackler was well known for her beautiful line drawings of the prominent dancers at the time, catching them live in motion during performance and rehearsals." The blending of text and illustration for this oversized book is a visual work of art ("the drawings are printed on specially-made paper, one side of the page only, and are handsomely suited for framing") and received high praise from critics. Richard Freis, in a review for the *Clarion-Ledger*, remarked upon Mara's "poetic" prose and called for her to be included among Mississippi's most notable writers: "Mississippi is justly famous for the many distinguished writers born within its borders. It has recently acquired another important writer by adoption, Thalia Mara, artistic director of the Jackson Ballet Guild."

In a column for the *Clarion-Ledger* appearing two weeks after Mara's death, writer Sherry Lucas, who interviewed Mara on several occasions during her time in Jackson, stated, with all explicit directness, that "Thalia Mara's death leaves a very big hole here," and that Mara's niece, Leanne Mahoney, will now serve as "keeper of her legacy" and "will take on the mantle," continuing the work of the Thalia Mara Arts International Foundation. Mahoney, a costume designer, worked for the Santa Fe Opera Company for thirty years before resigning her position in 1998 to move to Jackson to look after her aunt. She told Lucas, "I was around Thalia and my uncle Arthur Mahoney, and the world of theater opened up to me. . . . She became a mother and a mentor to me. She made the ultimate difference in my life. Any of her students will tell you the same thing."

One of those students was Madeleine Nichols, who was the former curator of the Jerome Robbins Dance Division at the New York Public Library for the Performing Arts from 1988 to 2005. She wrote the following for the publication of *On Pointe*, affirming what Mahoney related above:

> Thalia Mara looked for the best in you, she found it and then she expected you to always excel. Her attitude is conveyed in her writing, which is how I first "found" her. Then, when I was one of her summer students,

> she found something to encourage even when I could not see it. Imagine the irony, decades later, in my daily help to choreographers, dancers and others around the world, in a library devoted to dance, all because of her clear expectations. Thank you, Thalia!

Perhaps one of Mara's greatest honors was bestowed thirteen years after her death, a recognition that came from a nontraditional place: Innovate Mississippi, an organization whose mission is to "strengthen and grow the culture of innovation in Mississippi." For over twenty years they have encouraged and developed new companies and connected them with millions of dollars in seed and venture capital, resulting in new high-paying jobs being created within the state. In 2016 this organization announced their Mississippi Innovators Hall of Fame class of inductees, which included Mara. Tony Jeff, president of Innovate Mississippi, in recognizing Mara's legacy, highlighted how bringing the USA IBC to Jackson and establishing the World Performance Series had made a lasting economic impact on the state. Jeff wrote, "Her legacy, the USA IBC, continues as one of the most respected ballet competitions in the world, furthering the highest standards of ballet while contributing an economic impact of an estimated $12 million to Mississippi." She is not a typical innovator—"studies suggest that the average entrepreneur is in [his] forties," said Jeff—but Mara, who did not come to Mississippi until age sixty-five, devoted the last thirty years of her life creating projects that benefited the state, making her "an amazing innovator, for any age." Accepting the award on Mara's behalf was her niece, Leanne Mahoney, who told the audience:

> Thalia, throughout her life, cared about the human condition, the quality of life wherever she was. Especially here in Mississippi, her adopted home, and this is why I believe she would be especially pleased tonight, for your purpose in Innovate Mississippi is to encourage, with nurturing and resources, other creative thinkers with big ideas to persevere in realizing them.

Mara's contributions to the economic impact of the city and state cannot be overstated, but what Mara would most want to be remembered for is bringing the arts to others, here in Mississippi, in New York, and beyond. The greatest testament to her legacy and influence is the plethora of correspondence left behind, from former students and collaborators living all over the world, telling her about their latest projects, requesting her

Thalia Mara and David Keary. Photograph by Richard Finkelstein.

assistance with choreography, inviting her to serve on a panel, asking for her advice on an upcoming performance, or simply wishing her a "Merry Christmas" or "Happy Easter." The letters are personal, warm; they are evidence of a woman whose relationships were lasting and who successfully passed on her passion for dance to others in the US, Europe, Australia, New Zealand, and elsewhere. She was a teacher whose influence was felt long after the dance class was over.

Leanne Mahoney stated as much to interviewer Sherry Lucas: "The arts are of vital importance to [the] future of civilization. . . . There was just no question of that in her mind." Mara's friend Deborah Hilton agreed. Hilton wrote a letter to the *Clarion-Ledger* after the passing of her friend and shared, "[One] thing she often talked about with me was her concern for our culture. She thought it was important to hold beauty close to one's experience, that without a keen sense of what real beauty is, our society would fail." The Very Reverend Joseph O. Robinson included this sentiment in the final sentences of his eulogy when he said, "Thalia was unashamedly passionate, passionate about faith, passionate about beauty. She enjoyed, and we enjoyed with her, a beautiful life." But David Keary, artistic director of Ballet Mississippi, perhaps summed up Thalia Mara best: "She used to say, 'To dance, to live.' It was all about life with her."

Thalia Mara. Photograph by John F. Mahoney.
Courtesy of *Dance Teacher Now*.

Additional Tributes to Thalia Mara

Sandy McNeal, Mississippi artist and close friend of Mara's:

McNeal remembered meeting Thalia Mara on the balcony of the auditorium in Jackson now named for Mara. The two were introduced by former *Clarion-Ledger* writer Leslie Myers:

> We started talking and did not stop for the next thirteen years. . . . Her influence went way beyond art. . . . She had the ability to see the potential in others and felt it incumbent upon herself to give encouragement and a sort of command to pursue excellence.

Lynn Ware, mother of one of Mara's most successful ballet students:

> I first became involved with costuming because of my daughter's involvement with the Jackson Ballet. But the things I learned from Thalia—about aging and life in general—went way beyond ballet. I cannot imagine our lives without the influence of Thalia Mara.

Beth Ware Lytle, daughter of Lynn Ware and professional dancer, in a letter she wrote to Mara during her last illness:

> I am so grateful, Ms. Mara, for all you've given to me as a person as well as a dancer. I think of you often as I teach my students—they know you well.

Anna Fowler Blank, student at Jackson Ballet for six years, professional dancer and owner of her own dance studio in Santa Rosa Beach, Florida:

> [Thalia Mara] was my mentor, my friend, and my teacher. She was also one of the most spiritual, honest, and genuine people I've ever known. I will honor her memory always by modeling my teaching after hers.

CityDance Program, Jackson. Courtesy of USA IBC.

Afterword: The USA IBC Today

Though I only had the opportunity to meet Thalia Mara once, I often think about the energy and tenacity she must have had to get the city of Jackson and its citizens excited about having a two-week ballet competition, especially in a community that greatly favors sports and hunting. I am in awe of and so very grateful for the thousands of volunteers, hundreds of board members, and past leaders who have continued to carry the torch for nearly fifty years, making the USA International Ballet Competition one of the largest and most prestigious ballet competitions in the world.

Many things have changed since the first competition in 1979. I often run across typewritten letters and telegrams. It is amazing that communicating with leaders of other competitions around the globe is a simple email or Zoom call resulting in instant responses, rather than waiting months for a reply to a mailed, handwritten letter. Recruiting potential competitors is much easier thanks to the wonders of social media. Printed applications and marketing materials are a thing of the past.

Thalia would be proud to see that the USA IBC has grown and continued her dream of bringing high-quality arts programming to the South for all to experience. Through our outreach program, CityDance, thousands of children have been inspired and exposed to the arts. CityDance offers free ballet lessons to young students attending the Jackson Public Schools. Tickets to the competition and other ballet performances are made available to them and their families through the USA IBC.

The USA IBC past medalists and competitors have gone on to have storied careers that started in Jackson, Mississippi, onstage at Thalia Mara Hall: Nina Ananiashvili, José Manuel Carreño, and Brooklyn Mack, to name just a few. Many have come back to Jackson to participate in galas in between competitions. Lifelong friendships have been formed through the host-family volunteer program that matches competitors with a family that acts as their support system while in Jackson.

Though technology has greatly advanced the competition, many things remain the same. Quality, integrity, and high standards are certainly goals that Thalia Mara wanted for the competition, but southern hospitality is what she knew Mississippi had like nowhere else. Thalia has and continues to touch so many lives through the USA IBC. She left us this magnificent gift, and we now have the very important task of upholding her legacy both locally and internationally.

Mona Nicholas
Director of USA IBC

Portrait of Thalia Mara and Arthur Mahoney, ca. 1940. Courtesy of the estate of Thalia Mara.

Thalia Mara and Arthur Mahoney performing eighteenth-century traditional court dance. Courtesy of the estate of Thalia Mara.

Thalia Mara and Arthur Mahoney performing ballet, School of Ballet Repertory, New York. Courtesy of the estate of Thalia Mara.

Thalia Mara and Arthur Mahoney in traditional folk-dance costume. Photograph by Lewis Goren. Courtesy of the estate of Thalia Mara.

Close-up of Thalia Mara and Arthur Mahoney in eighteenth-century costumes. Courtesy of the estate of Thalia Mara.

Thalia Mara and Arthur Mahoney in costume. Courtesy of the estate of Thalia Mara.

Thalia Mara and Arthur Mahoney performing flamenco. Courtesy of the estate of Thalia Mara.

Thalia Mara and Arthur Mahoney clowning around, Martha's Vineyard. Courtesy of the estate of Thalia Mara.

Thalia Mara and Arthur Mahoney dancing at an informal gathering in their studio, New York. Courtesy of the estate of Thalia Mara.

Thalia Mara and Arthur Mahoney (*top first and second left*) enjoying friends and music in their home, New York. Courtesy of the estate of Thalia Mara.

Thalia Mara (*seated front left*), Lydia Newman (*standing left*), and Arthur Mahoney (*standing right*). Courtesy of the estate of Thalia Mara.

Thalia Mara and Arthur Mahoney sitting on floor with cat. Courtesy of the estate of Thalia Mara.

Thalia Mara at her birthday celebration. Courtesy of the estate of Thalia Mara.

Thalia Mara (*second left*) and William Kessler, president of the Jackson Ballet (*far right*), with dancers Mikhail Baryshnikov (*far left*) and Peter Martins (*second right*) leaving the Jackson airport. Baryshnikov and Martins were in Jackson to perform in the Benefit Ballet Gala on April 10, 1979, at the municipal auditorium, now known as Thalia Mara Hall. Courtesy of the estate of Thalia Mara.

Gene Kelly attending a party at Thalia Mara and Arthur Mahoney's studio, New York. This photo was taken after he became a famous Hollywood star, but he knew Thalia and Arthur when he was just starting out. His parents had owned a tap-dance school in Pennsylvania, and he had not studied any ballet before his arrival in New York City. When he was cast as a lead in the Broadway show *Pal Joey* (1940), he knew he needed training in ballet and went to Thalia and Arthur to study. Courtesy of the estate of Thalia Mara.

Thalia Mara and Todd Bolender (1914–2006). Bolender was an internationally renowned ballet dancer, teacher, choreographer, and director. For many years he was the artistic director of the Kansas City Ballet (1981–1995). Courtesy of the estate of Thalia Mara.

Thalia Mara with Todd Bolender. Courtesy of the estate of Thalia Mara.

Acknowledgments

First and foremost, I want and need to thank my dear friend Carla Wall, who has kept Thalia Mara's memory alive in my mind with her stories of their friendship. Without her, this book simply would not have happened. Second, I also would like to thank Leanne Mahoney, who was the first to document Thalia Mara's life. She created a website about Mara that I returned to repeatedly, and she organized much of her aunt's life in boxes that she left here in Jackson under Carla's care. Without those boxes, full of Mara's correspondence, contracts, personal photographs, and miscellany, I could not have completed this book. Thank you for entrusting me with telling Thalia's story and sharing additional books, photographs, scrapbooks, PowerPoint presentations, and personal anecdotes that I could not have obtained anywhere else. The precious materials both Carla and Leanne provided are the necessary foundation that a biographer depends upon to write an authentic life story. My deepest gratitude to both of you for holding on to these priceless treasures and granting me the opportunity to use them in this book.

And thanks to Mona Nicholas, director of the USA IBC. I remember you handing over so many materials at that first meeting in your office that allowed me to begin this biography. You made the research process as easy as I have ever had it! And with your fabulous staff—Ellen Treadway and Bailey Alexander—who answered my random questions and helped me find additional documents I did not have under less-than-ideal circumstances, I was able to complete this book. Thank you all for your support and contributions.

I also would like to thank librarians and others who helped me to flesh out Mara's story and life: April Berry, director of community engagement and education and academy faculty member, Kansas City Ballet; Chris Wydman, records manager and archivist, Wright State University; Norton Owen, director of preservation, Jacob's Pillow Dance Festival;

Brother Rogers, director of the programs and communication division, Mississippi Department of Archives and History; and Dale Stinchcomb, associate curator, Harvard Theatre Collection, Houghton Library, Harvard University.

At University Press of Mississippi, I would like to thank my "team": Valerie Jones, project editor; Linda Breslin, copyeditor; Pete Halverson, senior book designer; Craig Gill, director of University Press; and especially Jackson Watson, assistant to the director, who worked closely with Carla and me at the end on organizing all of the photographs and helping us obtain permissions. Several of you have worked with me on many or even all five of my books. Thank you for all of your hard work in making my books come to life. I am extremely proud to be associated with UPM.

Finally, thanks to my family: husband, Lus; sons, Will and Sam; and our dog, Oscar. I could not have written these books without your love and support, and Oscar, sitting in my chair beside me.

Appendix 1

Published Works

Thalia Mara was a prolific author, serving as a contributing editor to *Dance Magazine* from 1951 to 1956, and again from 1961 to 1965, and as a feature writer for the *Christian Science Monitor* from 1973 to 1975. In addition, she is the author of eleven books about dance, including textbooks for teachers and students at all levels of ballet. Her books were made available in English in the United States, England, India, and Australia, and several were translated and published in foreign-language editions. A list of titles, publishers, and foreign-language editions can be found below:

1955 *Do's and Don'ts of Basic Ballet Barre Work*, Dance Magazine

1956 *First Steps in Ballet: Basic Exercises at the Barre*, Doubleday (Republished in paperback by Dance Horizons in 1977)[41]

1957 *Do's and Don'ts of Basic Center Practice Work*, Dance Magazine (Reprinted in 2011 by Literary Licensing)

1957 *Second Steps in Ballet: Basic Center Exercises*, Doubleday (Republished in paperback by Dance Horizons in 1976)[42]

1958 *Third Steps in Ballet: Basic Allegro Steps*, Doubleday (Republished in paperback by Dance Horizons in 1976)[43]

1959 *Fourth Steps in Ballet: On Your Toes*, Doubleday (Republished in paperback by Dance Horizons in 1977)[44]

41. Also published in England, India, and Australia by Constable. Translated into German and published in Zurich, Switzerland, and Stuttgart, Germany, by Rascher Verlag. Translated into Spanish and published in Valencia, Spain, by Graficas Roman.

42. See note 1 above.

43. See note 1 above.

44. See note 1 above. Also translated into Arabic and published in Cairo, Egypt, by Dar Nahdet Misr.

1959 *Ballet: Home Practice for Beginners*, Longman Young Books

1959 *So You Want to Be a Ballet Dancer*, Pitman Publishing (Reprinted in 2011 by Literary Licensing)

1961 *Do's and Don'ts of Basic Allegro Work*, Dance Magazine (Reprinted in 2011 by Literary Licensing)

1966 *The Language of Ballet: An Informal Dictionary*, Cleveland World (Republished in paperback by Dance Horizons in 1976. Later reprints dropped the use of "informal" in the title: *The Language of Ballet: A Dictionary*.)

1976 *To Dance, to Live*, Dance Horizons (Republished in paperback by Dance Horizons in 1979)

Appendix 2

Choreographed Works and Featured and Soloist Performances

CHOREOGRAPHED WORKS

Principal choreographer for the Ballet Repertory Company
Principal choreographer for the Jackson Ballet Company

Major Works

The Nutcracker (full length), Tchaikovsky
Classical Symphony, Prokofiev
The Seasons, Glazunov
Ecole de Ballet, Shostakovich
Valse-fantaisie, Glinka
Scottish Fantasy, Mendelssohn
Schubertiad, Schubert
Boléro, Ravel
Point Counterpoint, Bach
Rhapsody in Blue, Gershwin
Nonet, Mozart

Operas and Operettas

Carmen, Bizet
La traviata, Verdi
Faust, Gounod

Babes in Toyland, Herbert
The Fortune Teller, Herbert
The Red Mill, Herbert
Rio Rita, Tierney

FEATURED DANCER AND SOLOIST PERFORMANCES

Featured Dancer

Capitol Theatre, New York
Radio City Music Hall, New York
Lewisohn Stadium, New York

Soloist

Ballet Suédois de Carina Ari, France and Touring
L'Opéra Privé de Paris, France and Touring
Fokine Ballet Company, New York

PERFORMANCES WITH ARTHUR MAHONEY

1936 *Carmen*, Lewisohn Stadium, New York
1939 *Carmen*, Lewisohn Stadium, New York
1939 Court Dances, Brooklyn Academy of Music, New York
1941 Spanish Folk Fiesta, Brooklyn Academy of Music, New York
1942 "Eighteenth-Century Court Dances," Jacob's Pillow, Massachusetts
1942 "Serenata Espanol," "Blue Fantasy," and "Jota Aragonese," Jacob's Pillow, Massachusetts
1943 "Boléro," "Cordoba," "Blues in the Night," "Echoes of Harlem," "Jota Aragonese," and "Gonna See My Gal," Jacob's Pillow, Massachusetts
1944 "Crosstown," Jacob's Pillow, Massachusetts
1944 Dance Recital with Thalia Mara, New York City Center, New York
1945 *Carmen*, Lewisohn Stadium, New York
1945 "Crosstown," "Serenade Espagnole," "Jota Aragonese," Jacob's Pillow, Massachusetts
1947 "Parnassus," "La Noche Clara," Jacob's Pillow, Massachusetts

Appendix 3

Major Honors and Awards

1990 Honorary Doctorate, Millsaps College

1990 Governor's Award for Excellence in the Arts

1990 Lifetime Achievement Award, Professional Dance Teachers' Association

1993 Mississippi Historical Society Award of Merit for Outstanding Contribution to Mississippi for "Planning of Mississippi Homecoming to Honor the 175th Anniversary of the State of Mississippi"

Thalia Mara Hall, Jackson. Courtesy of the estate of Thalia Mara.

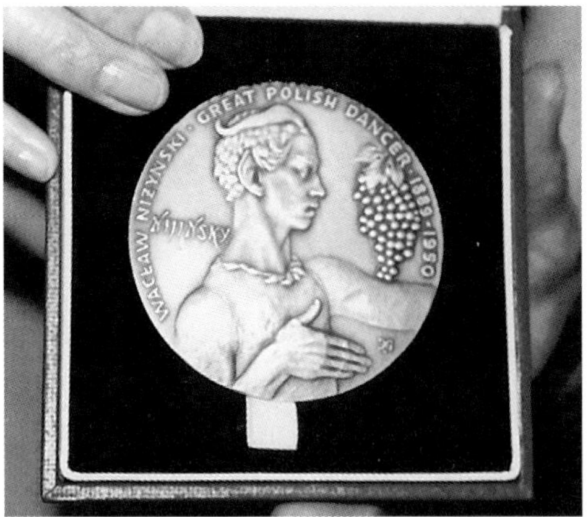

Vaslav Nijinsky Medal of Honor. Courtesy of the estate of Thalia Mara.

Mayor's Arts Achievement Honors Medal, Jackson, Mississippi. Courtesy of the estate of Thalia Mara.

Thalia Mara in cap and gown, Mississippi University for Women, Columbus, Mississippi. Courtesy of the estate of Thalia Mara.

MILLSAPS COLLEGE

To all to whom these presents shall come, greetings:

Be it known that

Thalia Mara

Performer and Teacher Whose Vision Created the U.S.A. International Ballet Competition and Brought Recognition to our Community, is given the title of

Doctor of Arts

and is hereby admitted to all the rights and privileges thereof.

Done at Millsaps College, Jackson, Mississippi this the twelfth day of May, nineteen hundred and ninety A.D.

Witness the seal of Millsaps College and signatures of the Faculty and Trustees hereunto affixed.

MILLSAPS COLLEGE MDCCCXCI

CHAIRMAN OF THE BOARD — PRESIDENT OF THE COLLEGE — DEAN OF THE COLLEGE

Honorary doctorate, Millsaps College, Jackson, May 12, 1990. Courtesy of the estate of Thalia Mara.

1994 *Dance Teacher Now* Circle of Dance Award for Lifetime Contributions to Dance Education

1994 Jackson Municipal Auditorium renamed Thalia Mara Hall

1994 Medal of Excellence awarded by Mississippi University for Women

1996 ALLY Lifetime Achievement Award, Arts Alliance of Jackson and Hinds County

1998 Mayor's Arts Achievement Honors

1998 Vaslav Nijinsky Medal of Honor, awarded by the government of Poland

Thalia Mara with Elise Winter (*front*), former first lady of Mississippi. Mara is being honored by the National Museum of Women in the Arts. Others pictured (*left to right*): Glady Lisanby, president of the Mississippi committee; Pat Fordice, first lady of Mississippi; and Wilhelmina Cole Holladay, founder and chair of the board of the National Museum of Women in the Arts. Courtesy of the estate of Thalia Mara.

1999 Blue Cross & Blue Shield of Mississippi Foundation Ageless Hero Award
2000 City of Jackson Best of the New South Award
2002 USA IBC Gold Medal for Artistic Achievement
2016 Inducted posthumously into the Mississippi Innovators Hall of Fame

OTHER RECOGNITIONS

Who's Who in American Women
Who's Who in the East
Who's Who in Mississippi
Foremost Women in Communication
State of Mississippi Eternal Flame Award for a Lifetime of Artistic Endeavor
Treasured Artist Award, Mississippi Committee of National Museum of Women in the Arts

Notes

Chapter 1: Early Life (1911–1929)

3 “I was speechless”: Mara, “Thalia Mara and Janet.”

3–4 “the most famous” and “she is always”: Hamilton, “It Happened in Texas.”

6 “the most exquisite” and “Prepare my swan”: Teeuwissen.

6 “Miss Butler had” and “This is hell”: Leanne Mahoney, “Thalia Mara Photo Gallery.”

7 “a great deal of” and “she deserved”: Leanne Mahoney, email to the author. 27 Mar. 2022.

7 “Through a twist”: Lyon.

9 “[her] real education”: Mara, “Thalia Mara and Janet.”

9, 12 “it became clear”: Lockspeiser.

13 “Ruth Page”: Josephine Schwarz, letter to Claudia and Grandpa.

13 “was one of the”: Laine.

13 “Dear old madame”: Josephine Schwarz, letter to Claudia and Grandpa.

14 “summer opera capital”: “History of Ravinia.”

14–15 “Dearest family”: Hermene Schwarz, letter to Schwarz family.

15 “Dearest Brother”: Josephine Schwarz, letter to brother.

16 “he looks just like” and “for the day”: Josephine Schwarz, letter to brother.

16 “Thalia told me”: Leanne Mahoney, email to the author. 27 Mar. 2022.

16 “on [Lydia’s] wedding night” and “very gentle and”: Leanne Mahoney, email to the author. 27 Mar. 2022.

16 “loving manner” and “drive”: Leanne Mahoney, email to the author. 27 Mar. 2022.

17 “found it difficult”: Leanne Mahoney, email to the author. 27 Mar. 2022.

17 “I came back”: Mara, “Thalia Mara and Janet.”

17–18 “stylized representation”: “What is Character Dance?”

18 “great gift,” “was her intelligence,” and “She was a”: Mara and Barringer 115.

18 “the director and”: Leanne Mahoney, “About Thalia.”

18, 20 “Fokine incorporated”: Isabelle Fokine.

20 “knowing them as”: Leanne Mahoney, email to the author. 27 Mar. 2022.

20 “We conducted”: Leanne Mahoney, email to the author. 31 Mar. 2022.

21 “For Arthur”: Leanne Mahoney, “About Thalia.”

21 “were stranded in”: DeMers.

22 “by the time” and “had found herself”: Leanne Mahoney, email to the author. 31 Mar. 2022.

22–23 "You kids," "At the British," and "developed quite": Leanne Mahoney, email to the author. 31 Mar. 2022.

23 "I do know" and "north of Rio": Leanne Mahoney, email to the author. 31 Mar. 2022.

Chapter 2: New York (1929–1940)

25–26 "until he was 18" and "That finished me": DeMers.

26 "You mean that" and "for six hours": DeMers.

26–27 "but it paid [his]" and "and had the added": DeMers.

27 "one night there": Leanne Mahoney, email to the author. 15 Apr. 2022.

27 "The ground floor": Leanne Mahoney, email to the author. 15 Apr. 2022.

28 "a traitor to": DeMers.

28 "I had to eat": "Thalia Mara," *Jackson Clarion-Ledger* 4B.

28 "the 16 Chester Hale": "Thalia Mara," *Jackson Clarion-Ledger* 4B.

28–29 "We had an aggressive" and "When I think of it": Myers, "Life's Grand Seeds" 6C.

29 "very difficult time" and "[she] was grateful": Mara, "Thalia Mara and Janet."

29 "you had to be": Mara, "Thalia Mara and Janet."

29 "early on, during," "from then on," and "legal name": Leanne Mahoney, email to the author. 15 Apr. 2022.

31 "During Thalia's time": Leanne Mahoney, email to the author. 15 Apr. 2022.

31 "a meeting that was" and "The impact of": Isabelle Fokine.

32 "In New York": Isabelle Fokine.

32 "the great genius": Mara, "Thalia Mara and Janet."

32 "all contemporary ballet": Mara, "Michel Fokine."

32–33 "Five Principles of Ballet Reform": Mara, "Michel Fokine."

33 "tutus and corset tops": Mara, "Thalia Mara and Janet."

33 "Isadora's insistence": Mara, "Michel Fokine."

33 "good composers": Mara, "Thalia Mara and Janet."

33 "In place": Michel Fokine.

33 "with indifference": Isabelle Fokine.

33 "it is as if": "Fokine, Michel."

33–34 "in the summer": Isabelle Fokine.

34 "A leading feature" and "after Bakst": Boudreau.

34 "performing ballet" and "Arthur, who choreographed": Mara and Barringer, *On Pointe* 118.

34 "Mara's dancing": "Thalia Mara," *Jackson Clarion-Ledger* 4B.

37–38 "Thalia Mara was my": Ed Mahoney.

Chapter 3: Teachers of Dance (1940–1973)

41 "So he thought": Mara, "Thalia Mara and Janet."

42 "Well, of course": Mara, "Thalia Mara and Janet."

43 "To acquire style": "Adventures in Style" 13.

43 "Though it is," "whether in solo," "brilliant," and "it is not often": "Adventures in Style" 35.

43–44 "Jacob's Pillow was": Boynton.

44 "was a financial" and "the diverse programming": "The Jacob's Pillow Story."
45 "many survived": Hamilton, "Rustic Life at Jacob's Pillow."
45 "the first performance": "The Jacob's Pillow Story."
45 "advocated a fitness": McPherson.
46 "At Jacob's Pillow": Underwood.
48 "Being that Thalia": Leanne Mahoney, email to the author. 22 Apr. 2022.
50 "mechanical approach," "Forgotten are," and "the large classes": Mara, "Style" 70–71.
52 "As far as I" and "I had started": Mara, "Thalia Mara and Janet."
53 "An academic ballet school" and "Incorporated under": "Dance School Plans."
54 "Working together": Mara, "Proposal to Establish a Pilot School."
54 "this was when": Leanne Mahoney, email to the author. 27 Mar. 2022.
54–55 "Basically, I" and "Discipline, determination,": Barringer 121.
55 "a good dancer," "How a child," and "great state-supported": Metcalfe 44.
57 "a skill which" and "to build manly": Metcalfe 44.
57 "Miss Mara" and "first professional": April Berry, personal interview. 1 Apr. 2021.
57–58 "We all had to" and "I respected": April Berry, personal interview. 1 Apr. 2021.
58 "Miss Mara was" and "beautiful and strong": April Berry, personal interview. 1 Apr. 2021.
59 "When I had the" and "To live is": April Berry, personal interview. 1 Apr. 2021.
59 "unique" and "here to stay": Metcalfe 44.

Chapter 4: Building Ballet in Mississippi (1973–1979)

62 "to manage a school" and "Ed Lydick called": Cora Jeanne Miller.
62 "When I was persuaded" and "We want to go": Mara, "Statement."
63 "I thought it a great pity" and "I knew it was a": Mara, "Statement."
63 "I decided that": Snow, "Choreographing a Dream" 2A.
64 "the first part" and "stunned students": Lucas, "Thalia" F1.
64 "I had to pin": Lucas, "Thalia" F2.
64 "I was used to": Snow, "Choreographing a Dream" 2A.
64 "Only three dancers": David Keary, personal interview. 16 June 2022.
64 "with most being": "Thalia Mara," *Jackson Clarion-Ledger* 4B.
64–65 "as [the group]": "Thalia Mara," *Jackson Clarion-Ledger* 4B.
65 "First, there existed": Mara, "Statement."
66 "There was such a": Jolly 18.
66 "Since the people": Jolly 19.
66 "Sixty-two dancers": Como.
67 "A lot of people": Wilson.
67 "Terry came to": Lindsay.
67 "People thought I": "Thalia Mara," *Jackson Clarion-Ledger* 4B.
67–68 "[After] the initial shock": Whittington.
68 "the most poetical": Mara, "Michel Fokine."
68–69 "It is abstract" and "The ballet was": Mara, "Michel Fokine."
69 "to increase ballet": "Thalia Mara," *Jackson Clarion-Ledger* 4B.
69 "The publicity for the": Wilson.
70 "Jackson has the": Wilson.
71 "not [being] merely part" and "[No] one individual": Henry.

71 "Because Jackson is a": Wilson.
72 "Dean of": Henry.
72–73 "For weeks," "for the most acrobatic," and "by the time": Keating 44, 49.

Chapter 5: The USA IBC and Other Projects (1979–1991)

76 "friendliness to the Russians": Hertzog 5.
76–77 "report," "Dear Mme. Azmi," "I'm writing this" and "many areas": Mara, letter to Mme. Azmi 1.
77 "The foremost problem," "wage scale," and "to heat the": Mara, letter to Mme. Azmi 1–3.
77 "very Russian," "I advised her," and "an International Arts": Hertzog 5.
77–78 "forced into," "without informing," and "Surely a": Mara, letter to Warren.
78 "A budget" and "Through much labor": Mara, letter to Warren.
79 "When I think back": "June 20–July 4, 1982."
80 "The loss of funding": "June 15–28, 1986."
80 "was as calm" and "Her perseverance": Lucas, "Thalia" F2.
81 "Top Twenty": "June 15–28, 1986."
81, 83 "Unlike last summer's" and "The Mississippi": Simpson 44, 49.
83–84 "Having for the past": Mara, "Personal Statement."
84 "It is a known": Mara, "Personal Statement."
84 "and to be drawn": Mara, "Personal Statement."
85 "Our links": Mara and Stern 21.
85 "very touched," "reflect[ed] the," and "many, many people": Myers, "Arts Awards" 2A.
85 "this money [wa]s to be": Mara, "Memo."
85–86 "As founder of this": Lobrano, letter to Ms. Thalia.
86 "The whole audience": Lucas, "ABT."
87 "was honored": John F. Mahoney, letter to Thalia Mara.
88 "Dear Thalia": Stevenson, letter to Thalia Mara.
88 "Dear Thalia Mara": Spohr, letter to Thalia Mara.
88 "How could it grow?": Wilson.
89 "Dance is not an": Wilson.

Chapter 6: The Thalia Mara Arts International Foundation (1991–1998)

92 "The mission of the": "Mission Statement."
93 "1. Sponsor and": "Mission Statement."
93 "filled to capacity": "June 18–July 2, 1994."
94 "It commemorates": "A Reception to Honor."
94 "continuing emphasis": "A Reception to Honor."
94–95 "I am rather," "It is a very," and "through the efforts": Simmons A1.
95 "successful operation," "poor students," and "upon graduation": Mara, "Proposal to Establish a Pilot School."
96 "Get humanities scholars": Mara, "Proposal to Establish a Pilot School."
96 "The school is": Lucas, "Thalia" F2.

96–97 "At a time": Weber.
97 "banner season": Lucas, "Jackson" 55.
98 "a lifetime of": Mississippi, Legislature, Senate.
98 "WHEREAS,": Mississippi, Legislature, Senate.
98 "petite powerhouse": "Thalia Mara," *Jackson Clarion-Ledger* 4B.
98 "Sell out": Carla Wall, email to the author. 24 May 2022.
99 "This [series]" and "I'm very excited": Snow, "Mara Foundation."
99–100 "One of my": Carla Wall, email to the author. 24 May 2022.
102 "I think the," "I wish," and "a working,": Lucas, "Thalia" F2.
102–3 "for her long" and "emotional ceremony": "June 15–30, 2002."

Chapter 7: Thalia Mara's Death and Legacy

105 "I was deeply": Iijima.
106 "Capezio is saddened": Gayle Miller.
106 "I'm so sorry": Alford.
106 "I am so sorry": Brown.
106 "We will miss": Nahat.
106 "one of" and "She was small": Pettus 1E.
106 "wonderful," "But, Thalia": Pettus 1E.
106 "driven": Pettus 1E.
107 "fine meals" and "She cooked": Pettus 2E.
107 "Thalia believed": Carla Wall, email to the author. 25 May 2022.
108 "She would get": Lucas, "Thalia" F2.
108 "There was only one": Robinson.
109 "Miss Mara's": Woody.
109 "future ballerinas": "Three Steps in Ballet."
109 "a masterpiece": Wyndham.
110 "As a teacher": Philp.
110 "The bones of a": Mara, "Foreword: To Parents" vii.
110–11 "at least four or," "there have been," "three distinct schools," and "the teacher to whom": Mara, "Foreword: To Parents" vii–ix.
111 "began as a" and "Many coaches": Mara, "Foreword: To Parents" xi.
111–12 "My great desire": "International Ballet Competition" 26.
112 "the great need" and "for the standardization": Mara, foreword, *The Language of Ballet* v.
112 "it is not": Mara, foreword, *The Language of Ballet* v.
113 "Mackler was well known": Leanne Mahoney, email to the author. 24 Mar. 2022.
113 "the drawings are": Freis 1.
113 "poetic" and "Mississippi is": Freis 1.
113 "Thalia Mara's death," "keeper" and "will take on": Lucas, "Keeping."
113 "I was around": Lucas, "Keeping."
113–14 "Thalia Mara looked for the": Nichols.
114 "strengthen and grow": Jeff.
114 "Her legacy," "studies suggest," and "an amazing": Jeff.
114 "Thalia, throughout": Leanne Mahoney, email to the author. 24 Mar. 2022.
115 "The arts": Lucas, "Keeping."

115 “[One] thing she”: Hilton.
115 “Thalia was unashamedly”: Robinson.
115 “She used to”: Gaitanoglou.

Additional Tributes to Thalia Mara

117 “We started talking”: “A Tribute to Thalia.”
117 “I first became involved”: “A Tribute to Thalia.”
117 “I am so grateful”: “A Tribute to Thalia.”
117 “[Thalia Mara] was my mentor”: “A Tribute to Thalia.”

Bibliography

"The 1996 ALLY Awards." 19 Sept. 1996. USA IBC Archives.

"About the Author." *Steps in Ballet*, Princeton Book Publishers, 2004, pp. 174–76.

"About Us." *USA International Ballet Competition*, www.usaibc.com/ about-us/. Accessed 31 Mar. 2021.

"Adventures in Style: Interviewing Arthur Mahoney, Expert Stylist of the Dance." *Dance Magazine*, vol. 17, no. 5, Apr. 1943, pp. 13+.

Alford, Marcus. Letter to Sue Lobrano. 13 Oct. 2003. USA IBC Archives.

"Anna Pavlowa and Her Ballet Russe." Chicago: Medinah Temple, 4 Dec. 1920.

Barringer, Janice. "A Look at the USA International Ballet Competition." *On Pointe: Basic Pointe Work and a Look at the USA International Ballet Competition*, Princeton Book Publishers, 2005, pp. 73–125.

Bloom, Ronna. Letter to Thalia Mara. 5 Feb. 1990. USA IBC Archives.

Boudreau, Leo. *Leon Bakst's Costume Design for a Satyr in "Cleopatra" (1910)*. 1 Sept. 2013, *Flickr*, www.flickr.com/photos/57440551@N03/9661385822. Accessed 15 Mar. 2021.

Boynton, Andrew. "There's No Place Like Jacob's Pillow." *New Yorker*, 16 June 2012, www.newyorker.com/culture/culture-desk/theres-no-place-like-jacobs-pillow. Accessed 14 July 2020.

Brown, Glenda. Letter to Sue Lobrano. 14 Oct. 2003. USA IBC Archives.

"A Celebration of Life: Thalia Mara, June 28, 1911 to October 8, 2003." 11 Oct. 2003. USA IBC Archives.

Como, William. "History of Ballet Competitions." June 1990.

Crabb, Michael. "Arnold Spohr: Dancer and Inspirational Ballet Director who Worked with Fonteyn, Markova, and Baryshnikov." *The Independent*, 13 May 2010. Accessed 23 July 2020.

Dahlburg, John-Thor. "A Center of Culture in Catfish Country, Thanks to Miss Mara." *Los Angeles Times*, 14 Dec. 2003, p. A20. USA IBC Archives.

"Dance School Plans Academic Subjects." *New York Times*, 14 Sept. 1963. Accessed 1 Apr. 2021.

DeMers, John. "Arthur Mahoney Tells of His Fantastic Career: From Boxer, Ballplayer, Cowboy, to World of Glittering Ballet." *UPI Archives*, 5 Sept. 1982. Accessed 15 Mar. 2021.

Dunning, Jennifer. "Thalia Mara, 92, Ballet Educator." *New York Times*, 11 Oct. 2003. Accessed 17 June 2020.

Eldin, Dina Salah. "Burning Down the House: Artistic Freedom under Fire in Egypt." *NPR*, 16 June 2013, www.npr.org.

Fokine, Isabelle. "Biography." *Fokine Estate-Archive*, www.michelfokine.com/id4.html. Accessed 16 Mar. 2021.

Fokine, Michel. "Fokine's Revolutionary Platform—Sent to the Imperial Theatre Directors 1904." *Fokine Estate-Archive*, www.michelfokine.com/id63.html. Accessed 16 Mar. 2021.

"Fokine, Michel." *Encyclopedia.com*, www.encyclopedia.com/people/literature-and-arts/dance-biographies/michel-fokine. Accessed 8 July 2021.

"Founder: Thalia Mara." *USA International Ballet Competition*, www.usaibc.com/the-competition/founder-thalia-mara/. Accessed 17 June 2020.

Freis, Richard. "Ballet Guild Director's Book 'A Celebration.'" *Jackson Clarion-Ledger*, 13 Dec. 1977, p. 1.

Gaitanoglou, Joanna. "Arts Patron Thalia Mara Dies at 92." *WLBT*, 9 Oct. 2003, www.wlbt.com. Accessed 14 July 2020.

Hamilton, Caroline. "It Happened in Texas: Anna Pavlova." *ACTX: Arts and Culture Texas*, 10 Sept. 2020. Accessed 9 Mar. 2021.

Hamilton, Caroline. "These Vintage 1941 Photos Show Rustic Life at Jacob's Pillow, and the Star Dancers Who Saved It." *Pointe*, 28 July 2017, pointemagazine.com/these-vintage-1941-photos-show-rustic-life-at-jacobs-pillow-and-the-star-dancers-who-saved-it/. Accessed 14 July 2020.

Harmon, George. Letter to Thalia Mara. 22 Feb. 1990. USA IBC Archives.

Henry, John B., III. "Introduction." *Dance Image: A Tribute to Serge Diaghilev*, International Ballet Competition Program, June 1979, Jackson, Mississippi. USA IBC Archives.

Hertzog, Joan. "Jackson Ballet Director to Egypt." *Capital Reporter*, 29 Jan. 1981, p. 5.

Hilton, Deborah. "Thalia Mara Had Vision for the Future." *Jackson Clarion-Ledger*.

"History of Ravinia." *Ravinia Festival*, www.ravinia.org/Page/History. Accessed 12 Mar. 2021.

"Hold the Moment." *Dance Teacher Now*, May 1990, pp. 16–17.

Iijima, Takashi. "Re: Thalia Mara." Received by Sue Lobrano, 31 Oct. 2003. USA IBC Archives.

"Innovators Hall of Fame Inducts Thalia Mara." *USA International Ballet Competition*, 11 Oct. 2016, www.usaibc.com/2016/10/11/innovators-hall-of-fame-inducts-thalia-mara/. Accessed 31 Mar. 2022.

"International Ballet Competition: Thalia Mara." *Belhaven College Magazine*, vol. 11, no. 1, Aug. 2002, p. 26.

"The Jacob's Pillow Story." *Jacob's Pillow Dance*, www.jacobspillow.org/about/pillow-history/jacobs-pillow-story/. Accessed 14 July 2020.

Jeff, Tony. "Thalia Mara was an Innovator." *Jackson Clarion-Ledger*, 18 Nov. 2016. Accessed 13 July 2020.

Jennings, Luke. "Sergei Diaghilev: First Lord of the Dance." *The Guardian*, 11 Sept. 2010. Accessed 23 July 2020.

Jolly, Bettye. "Jacksonians 1977: Thalia Mara." *Jackson Magazine*, Jan. 1978, pp. 18–19. USA IBC Archives.

"June 18–29, 1979." *USA International Ballet Competition*, www.usaibc.com/the-competition/. Accessed 31 Mar. 2021.

"June 20–July 4, 1982." *USA International Ballet Competition*, www.usaibc.com/the-competition/. Accessed 31 Mar. 2021.

"June 15–28, 1986." *USA International Ballet Competition*, www.usaibc.com/the-competition/. Accessed 31 Mar. 2021.

"June 17–July 1, 1990." *USA International Ballet Competition*, www.usaibc.com/the-competition/. Accessed 19 Apr. 2021.

"June 18–July 2, 1994." *USA International Ballet Competition*, www.usaibc.com/the-competition/. Accessed 23 Apr. 2021.

"June 15–30, 2002." *USA International Ballet Competition*, www.usaibc.com/the-competition/. Accessed 11 Aug. 2021.

Keary, David. "Our Organization." *Ballet Mississippi*, 2020, balletms.com/our-organization/. Accessed 25 Mar. 2021.

Keating, Bern. "Mississippi Pas de Deux." *Signature Magazine*, Dec. 1979, pp. 42–49.

Laine, Barry. "Dance Begins to Flourish in Chicago." *New York Times*, 18 July 1982. Accessed 12 Mar. 2021.

Lindsay, Virgi. "Thalia Mara's Vision Lands IBC in Jackson." *Jackson Clarion-Ledger*, 7 June 1998. USA IBC Archives.

Lobrano, Sue. "Ballet Educator Thalia Mara Dies at 92." USA International Ballet Competition, 7 Oct. 2003. USA IBC Archives.

Lobrano, Sue. Letter to Ms. Thalia Mara. 18 Oct. 1988. USA IBC Archives.

Lockspeiser, Edward. "Serge Diaghilev: Russian Ballet Impresario." *Encyclopedia Britannica*, www.britannica.com/biography/Serge-Pavlovich-Diaghilev. Accessed 11 Mar. 2021.

Lucas, Sherry. "ABT with Carreño Is a Can't-Miss Combo in This Town." *Jackson Clarion-Ledger*, 9 Nov. 1999. USA IBC Archives.

Lucas, Sherry. "Jackson Labeled 'Cultural Mecca.'" *Jackson Clarion-Ledger*, 28 Feb. 1999, p. 55. USA IBC Archives.

Lucas, Sherry. "Keeping Mara's Flame Alive and Bright." *Jackson Clarion-Ledger*, 21 Oct. 2003. USA IBC Archives.

Lucas, Sherry. "Thalia: At 89, Still a Force in Jackson's Art." *Jackson Clarion-Ledger*, 18 Feb. 2001, pp. F1–F2. USA IBC Archives.

Lyon, Jeff. "Oh, Did They Dance!" *Chicago Tribune*, 28 Jan. 1996. Accessed 10 Mar. 2021.

Mahoney, Ed. "Re: Thalia Mara." Received by Sue Lobrano, 17 Oct. 2003. USA IBC Archives.

Mahoney, John F. Letter to Thalia Mara. 14 Aug. 1991. USA IBC Archives.

Mahoney, Leanne. "About Thalia." *Thalia Mara*, www.thaliamara.com/about_thalia.html. Accessed 13 July 2020.

Mahoney, Leanne. "Thalia Mara Photo Gallery." *Thalia Mara*, www.thaliamara.com/galleryD8.html. Accessed 13 July 2020.

Mara, Thalia. "A Brief History of the Thalia Mara Arts International Foundation." The Collection of Thalia Mara.

Mara, Thalia. Curriculum Vitae. USA IBC Archives.

Mara, Thalia. Foreword. *The Language of Ballet: A Dictionary*, Princeton Book Publishers, 1987, p. v.

Mara, Thalia. "Foreword: To Parents." *Steps in Ballet*, Princeton Book Publishers, 2004, pp. vii–xi.

Mara, Thalia. Letter to Mme. Azmi. 17 Jan. 1981. USA IBC Archives.

Mara, Thalia. Letter to Warren E. Ludlam, Jr. 20 Mar. 1981. USA IBC Archives.

Mara, Thalia. Life Summary. USA IBC Archives.

Mara, Thalia. "Memo to the Executive Committee of Mississippi Ballet International Inc." 18 Oct. 1988. USA IBC Archives.

Mara, Thalia. "Michel Fokine and *Les Sylphides*." *The Jackson Ballet Guild Presents the Jackson Ballet*, 31 Mar. 1977. USA IBC Archives.

Mara, Thalia. "Personal Statement Regarding the 1989 International Arts Festival for Peace." USA IBC Archives.

Mara, Thalia. "Project: Increase the Influence of the USA International Ballet Competition Locally, Nationally, and Internationally." USA IBC Archives.

Mara, Thalia. "Proposal to Establish a Pilot School Testing a Curriculum Integrating the Arts and the Humanities with the Academic Curriculum." USA IBC Archives.

Mara, Thalia. "Statement." USA IBC Archives.

Mara, Thalia. *Steps in Ballet*. Princeton Book Publishers, 2004.

Mara, Thalia. "Style: Lost Element in American Ballet?" *Dance Magazine*, 5 May 1960, pp. 70–71.

Mara, Thalia. "Thalia Mara and Janet Baker-Carr." Interview by Janet Baker-Carr. *Conversations*, no. 102, Mississippi Public Broadcasting. *American Archive of Public Broadcasting*, www.americanarchive.org/catalog/cpb-aacip-60-80ht7fj1. Accessed 22 Apr. 2022.

Mara, Thalia, and Janice Barringer. *On Pointe: Basic Pointe Work and a Look at the USA International Ballet Competition*. Princeton Book Publishers, 2005.

Mara, Thalia, and Tina Mackler. *To Dance, to Live*. Dance Horizons, 1977.

Mara, Thalia, and Alfred Stern. "1989 International Arts Festival for Peace." July 1987, pp. 1–21. USA IBC Archives.

"The Mayor's Arts Achievement Honors in Tribute to Thalia Mara, Margaret Walker Alexander, and Eudora Welty." 30 July 1998. USA IBC Archives.

McLeod, Marilyn. *Adolph Rudolphovich Bolm*. 2002, www.adolphbolm.com. Accessed 11 Mar. 2021.

McPherson, Elizabeth. "Joseph H. Pilates." *Dance Teacher*, dance-teacher.com/joseph-h-pilates/. Accessed 14 July 2020.

Metcalfe, Jack. "Ballet School Dwells on Other Graces Too." *Daily News*, 23 Apr. 1968, p. 44. USA IBC Archives.

Miller, Cora Jeanne. "History of Jackson Ballet." 27 Aug. 2014. USA IBC Archives.

Miller, Gayle. "Re: promised!" Received by Sue Lobrano, 31 Oct. 2003. USA IBC Archives.

"Mission Statement and Five Year Goals." Thalia Mara Arts International Foundation newsletter. USA IBC Archives.

Mississippi, Legislature, Senate. Thalia Mara; commend. *Mississippi Legislature*, http://billstatus.ls.state.ms.us/documents/1998/SC/SC0649PS.htm. Mississippi Legislature, 1998 regular session, Senate Concurrent Resolution 649, adopted 24 Mar. 1998.

"Miss Thalia Mara." *The Jackson Ballet Guild Presents the Jackson Ballet*, 31 Mar. 1977. USA IBC Archives.

Moses, Jennifer. "Royal Splendor in the Deep South." *New York Times*, 3 June 2001.

Myers, Leslie. "Arts Awards for Lifetime Achievement." *Jackson Clarion-Ledger*, 7 Mar. 1990, pp. 2A+.

Myers, Leslie. "Life's Grand Seeds Continue to Sprout for Lady of Dance." *Jackson Clarion-Ledger*, 27 Dec. 1983, pp. 6A–6C.

Nahat, Dennis. "Re: Thalia." Received by Sue Lobrano, 10 Oct. 2003. USA IBC Archives.

Nichols, Madeleine. "Quotes on Thalia Mara." *Thalia Mara*, www.thaliamara.com/about_thalia.html. Accessed 31 Mar. 2022.

Pettus, Gary. "Thalia Mara." *Jackson Clarion-Ledger*, 10 Oct. 2003, pp. 1E–2E. USA IBC Archives.

Philp, Richard. "Remembering Thalia." *Thalia Mara*, http://www.thaliamara.com/article_b.html. Accessed 13 July 2020.

"Radio City Music Hall Corps de Ballet." *Dancers Over 40*, dancersover40.org/rcmh.shtml. Accessed 16 Mar. 2021.

"A Reception to Honor Thalia Mara, Recipient of the *Dance Teacher Now* 1994 Circle of Dance Award." *Dance Teacher Now*, 28 June 1994. USA IBC Archives.

"Rex Cooper is Dead; Dancer Led Ballet." *New York Times*, 31 Oct.1970. Accessed 25 Mar. 2021.

Robinson, Joseph O. "Thalia Mara: Eulogy." *Thalia Mara: A Celebration of Life*. 11 Oct. 2003.

Schwarz, Hermene. Letter to Schwarz family. 1925. Josephine Schwarz Papers, Special Collections and Archives, University Libraries, Wright State University, Dayton, Ohio, series III, MS 218, box 14, folder 11. 5 Aug. 2020.

Schwarz, Josephine. Letter to brother. 1925. Josephine Schwarz Papers, Special Collections and Archives, University Libraries, Wright State University, Dayton, Ohio, series III, MS 218, box 14, folder 11. 5 Aug. 2020.

Schwarz, Josephine. Letter to Claudia and Grandpa. July 1925. Josephine Schwarz Papers, Special Collections and Archives, University Libraries, Wright State University, Dayton, Ohio, series III, MS 218, box 14, folder 11. 5 Aug. 2020.

Simmons, Grace. "City Auditorium Gets New Name: Thalia Mara Hall." *Jackson Clarion-Ledger*, 1994, p. A1.

Simpson, Herbert M. "Gold Rush on the Mississippi." *Dance Magazine*, Oct. 1986, pp. 42–49.

Snow, Donnie. "Mara Foundation Bringing More Arts to Jackson." *Jackson Clarion-Ledger*, 29 July 1999.

Snow, Donnie. "Thalia Mara: Choreographing a Dream." *Jackson Clarion-Ledger*, 30 July 1999, p. 2A.

Sorell, Walter. "Book Reviews: *To Dance, to Live*." *Dance News*, Jan. 1978.

Spohr, Arnold. Letter to Thalia Mara. 26 July 1990. USA IBC Archives.

Stevenson, Ben. Letter to Thalia Mara. 22 July 1990. USA IBC Archives.

Teeuwissen, Jon. "Four Minutes and a Dying Swan: Anna Pavlova and Becoming the Symbol of the New Russian Ballet." *Michigan Opera Theatre*, 8 July 2020. Accessed 11 Mar. 2021.

"Thalia Mara." *Jackson Clarion-Ledger*, 11 Oct. 2003, p. 4B. USA IBC Archives.

"Thalia Mara." World Series Performance. 22 Jan. 2003. USA IBC Archives.

"Thalia Mara." *San Diego Union-Tribune*, 14 Oct. 2003. *Legacy.com*, www.legacy.com/us/obituaries/sandiegouniontribune/name/thalia-mara-obituary?pid=1478338. Accessed 14 July 2020.

"Thalia Mara, Artistic Director, USA International Ballet Competition." USA IBC Archives.

"Three Steps in Ballet." *Pensacola (FL) News Journal*, 10 Nov. 1957.

Treppendahl, Katherine. "Thalia Mara." *Mississippi Encyclopedia*, 11 July 2017. Accessed 13 July 2020.

"A Tribute to Thalia Mara—A Great Lady." USA IBC Archives.

Trigg, Brenda. "Kit Whitsett Fields Is 2018 USA IBC Official Artist." *USA International Ballet Competition*, 22 Aug. 2017.

Underwood, Sharry. "Turning Exercise on Its Head: A Memory of Joe Pilates." *Dance Magazine*, 20 Dec. 2010, www.dancemagazine.com/turning-exercise-on-its-head/. Accessed 20 Apr. 2021.

"USA IBC Announces 1998 Economic Impact." *Dance Magazine*, Jan. 1999. USA IBC Archives.

Weber, Bruce. "Sport Meets Art at an International Competition in Mississippi." *New York Times*, 27 June 1998. USA IBC Archives.

"What Is Character Dance?" *Temecula Ballet*, www.temeculaballet.com/folkloric-character-dance/. Accessed 12 Mar. 2021.

Whittington, Mary Jayne. "In the Beginning: Thalia Mara." *Jackson Magazine*, June 1979. USA IBC Archives.

Wilson, Chrissy. Interview with Thalia Mara. *Artsnews*, Spring 1990. USA IBC Archives.

Woody, Regina J. "Step by Step." *New York Times*, 19 July 1959.

Wyndham, Lee. "For Ballet Students." *Morristown (NJ) Daily Record*, 14 Sept. 1956.

Index

Page numbers in **boldface** indicate illustrations.

Photo credit: Imani Khayyam

Carolyn J. Brown is a teacher, writer, editor, and independent scholar who now resides in Chapel Hill, North Carolina, after living in Jackson, Mississippi, for sixteen years. Brown graduated from Duke and UNC-Greensboro, where she earned both her master's and PhD. She has written four books: the award-winning biographies *A Daring Life: A Biography of Eudora Welty* (2012) and *Song of My Life: A Biography of Margaret Walker* (2014); *The Artist's Sketch: A Biography of Painter Kate Freeman Clark* (2017); and her most recent book, *A de Grummond Primer: Highlights of the Children's Literature Collection* (2021). Find her at www.carolynjbrown.net.

Photo credit: Carlton Wall

Carla S. Wall, a consultant in communications and public relations, has demonstrated a lifelong commitment to the arts, serving on boards for theater, visual arts, ballet, and community organizations. She edited *Art to Life: Welty and Theatre* by distinguished art historian Patti Carr Black. She holds a master's degree from the University of Virginia.